# OUTCASTS:

## The Image of Journalists in Contemporary Film

by
HOWARD GOOD

The Scarecrow Press, Inc.
Metuchen, N.J., & London
1989

The author gratefully acknowledges permission to reprint the following:

Excerpts from "Little Gidding" in *Four Quartets* by T.S. Eliot, copyright 1943 by T.S. Eliot; renewed 1971 by Esme Valerie Eliot. Reprinted by permission of Harcourt Brace Jovanovich, Inc. and by Faber and Faber Ltd. Publishers.

Lines from "The Second Coming" are reprinted with permission of Macmillan Publishing Company from *Collected Poems* of W.B. Yeats. Copyright 1922 by Macmillan Publishing Company, renewed 1952 by Bertha Georgie Yeats. Also by permission of A.P. Watt Ltd. on behalf of Michael B. Yeats and Macmillan London Ltd.

Lines from "Imagine," Words and Music by John Lennon. © 1971 LENONO MUSIC. All Rights Controlled and Administered by Blackwood Music, Inc. All Rights Reserved. International Copyrights Secured. Used by permission.

Photographs courtesy of The Museum of Modern Art.

British Library Cataloguing-in-Publication data available.

**Library of Congress Cataloging-in-Publication Data**

Good, Howard, 1951–
Outcasts : the image of journalists in contemporary film / by Howard Good.
p. cm.
Bibliography: p.
Includes index.
ISBN 0-8108-2162-1
1. Journalists in motion pictures. 2. Motion pictures—United States. I. Title.
PN1995.9.J6G58 1989
791.43′09′093520—dc19 88-7688

To my children,
Gabriel, Graham, and Brittany

"The little ones leaped & shouted & laugh'd
And all the hills echoed."

Andrea: Unhappy is the land that breeds no hero.
Galileo: No, Andrea. Unhappy is the land that needs a hero.

—Bertolt Brecht, *Galileo*

I don't read the paper and I don't listen to the radio neither. I know the world's been shaved by a drunken barber, and I don't have to read it.

—The "Colonel" (Walter Brennan), *Meet John Doe*

Journalists! … A lot of lousy, daffy buttinskis swelling around with holes in their pants, borrowing nickels from office boys.

—Hildy Johnson, *The Front Page*

# CONTENTS

# PREFACE

IT TAKES SO LONG to plan, research, write, and revise even a small book that when the book is finally finished, nothing—neither you nor the world—is the same as it was when you started. While I was working on *Outcasts,* my daughter was born, U.S. planes raided the Libyan capital of Tripoli, a sculpturesque ash tree blew down in the yard during a freak October snowstorm, the Iran-contra scandal broke, *Platoon* opened to excellent reviews, interest rates rose, dropped, and then rose again, and our goldfish, Zippy, died.

The very process of writing changes you in subtle but substantial ways. "Writing," Pulitzer Prize-winner Donald M. Murray said, "is an act of arrogance and communication." And discovery, he might have added. The book you envisioned writing isn't necessarily the one you write. Between the conception and the execution, to adapt a trope of T.S. Eliot's, falls the shadow of your own personality. Spend enough late nights struggling at your desk, and you discover things about yourself—about your passions and prejudices, your fantasies and flaws—that you would as soon leave undiscovered.

I don't want to make too much of my travails in writing this book (actually, I do, but I am fighting the impulse). To be sure, I had moments of exhilaration, when words and ideas seemed to coalesce into luminous patterns. But more often I had moments of doubt and anxiety, and now that it is all over, I wonder whether I should have used so personal, and occasionally hypercritical, a tone; whether anyone will read what I have written; and if anyone does, whether he or she will empathize with my point of view. Once published, a book is launched on a haphazard voyage, like a time capsule sent rocketing into deep space on the off chance that someone or something is out there in the vast blackness to receive and decipher its contents.

Perhaps I am overdramatizing. No one really writes a book alone. Others are invariably implicated in the crime. I have drawn on dozens of writers for facts and arguments and inspiration. I have benefited from a grant from the Research Foundation of the State University of New York. Most of all, I have had the love and understanding of my family. I wish to officially thank my children, especially Graham, who would ask when I emerged bleary-eyed from my basement study if the "tractor" (he meant chapter) was done yet, and I wish to humbly thank my wife, Barbara. She has been teacher, editor, proofreader, fan, and friend—the cone of light shining down on the page as I wrote.

Howard Good

# DREAMING IN HEADLINES

Movies matter.—Steven Bach,
*Final Cut*

ON RAINY SATURDAYS when I was 11 and 12 years old, my friends and I would escape to the movies. It didn't much matter what was playing. Almost any movie was better than moping around the house and having your mother yell at you to go read a book. Admission to the Gables was 35 cents, cheap even by the standards of the early 1960s. The purple plush on the seats had long since faded to a memory, and the floor was permanently sticky from generations of children spilling candy and soda. We would stuff ourselves with Jujubes, Snowcaps, popcorn, and frozen Milky Ways, and watch spellbound as a giant prehistoric reptile trampled Tokyo or as two cowboys faced each other in the middle of a dusty street and reached for their guns. Violence stirred our prepubescent imaginations, and walking home under the dripping trees, we would pause to reenact the shoot-outs and fist fights we had just seen on the screen.

The Gables, and the ancient usherette who patrolled the darkness with a flashlight and fixed scowl, are gone now. On the corner where the theater stood is a strip mall. But the movies I saw while I was growing up cut grooves in my mind, like the notches on the revolver of a gunfighter, and mysteriously shaped the man I have become. Before I was old enough to find out about life for myself, movies were my tutor, offering glimpses of love and work and bravery and death. My first impressions of the world beyond my immediate experience came from film (and TV), and they may have been the most lasting.

I was nominally an adult—24, married, and in graduate school—when I saw *All the President's Men* (1976). If I had seen a newspaper film before then, I don't remember it. Anyway, I thrilled to reporters fighting corruption as I had once thrilled to cowboys fighting Indians. I was among the record 50,000 students who were enrolled in journalism schools after Watergate, and I had never set foot inside a newsroom. The film showed journalism as I wanted it to be, epochal and exciting. I think that it must have confirmed my decision to pursue a newspaper career.

By the time *Absence of Malice* (1981) was released, I was an assistant national editor on a morning paper in the South. I felt more than affronted, I felt baffled and betrayed, by the film's antagonistic portrayal of the press. I couldn't recognize myself or my colleagues in the characters on the screen, but what was there to prevent an uninformed public from identifying all journalists with vultures like Megan Carter and Mac? Only after I had said goodbye to daily journalism, and to the reflex reaction that every attack on newspapers was an attack on the foundations of freedom, did I begin to realize that anti-press films might reveal something beside Hollywood's treachery and irresponsibility. A feature film, Charles Maland wrote, "must reinforce the cultural values and attitudes of its viewers if it expects to be popular."[1] Filmmakers don't lead public opinion; they usually follow it, or try to. The narrative patterns of the journalism film genre are mirrors of, and metaphors for, the relationship between the public and the press, its ruined hopes, desperate wishes, and ambiguous promises.

Yet little has been written about the genre, only one book, *Stop the Presses!: The Newspaperman in American Films* (1976) by Alex Barris, and a scattering of newspaper and magazine articles. And Barris' book is, to put it politely, inadequate to the subject. Like too many of the genre studies I read in preparing my own, it is an exhaustive—and, finally, exhausting—catalog, long on film titles, release dates, and the names of stars, writers, and directors, but short on context and analysis.[2] To be able to explore the symbols and concerns that lie behind the titles, and still keep my study to manageable dimensions, I have focused on representative films from the 1960s to the 1980s. Of overriding interest to me is how the working life of the journalist has been allegorized on the screen, and so I have discussed for the most part films that deal specifically with reporters and editors in their professional roles. I have left out the sort of love stories and family melodramas that Barris included in his chapter, "The Reporter As Human Being." The films that invoke the pivotal myths of the genre are precisely those in which news people have been portrayed as something more, or less, than human.

There is no discussion in the following pages of the "grammar of film" either. Analyses of camera angles, lighting, and other film techniques clearly have their place, but my study isn't it. I might as well admit here that my emphasis is more on journalism than on film. My formal training in film amounts to one college course, which I took 15 years ago and in which I got—I might as well admit this, too, while I am in a confessional mode—a D. I offer in excuse that the films we saw weren't very good. One opened with a long shot of an empty room, slowly went to a medium shot, and ended with a close-up of a small, framed photograph of waves that was hanging on the wall. Nothing else happened for an hour and a half except that I grew profoundly bored.

Most people attend films to enjoy stories, and I have interpreted journalism films on the basis of the stories they tell. These begin with a journalist whose professional loyalties put him in conflict with society. He then is plunged into a crisis of conscience by a tragedy resulting from his overzealous reporting. Or he undergoes a test of his commitment and skill as he battles to expose a corrupt social order. Both struggles are paths to his eventual reintegration into the community. The formula takes many guises, but it is always an elegy for lost innocence and a rite of redemption, and viewers vicariously participate in the ceremonies and psalms.

The typical genre study assumes that filmmaking is myth-making, and that the myths derive from inherent human impulses and address certain universal experiences.[3] "The narrative of genre film is mythic," Vivian

Sobchack, for example, stated, "and its various forms of expression in the individual genres are comparable to the discrete rituals through which myth is often articulated."[4] Yet genres evolve, and they evolve in culturally specific ways. The journalism films of the past quarter century had to accommodate shifts in public opinion and the tides of history to continue to attract audiences. This was a period of violent talk and equally violent change, when faith in man and God and institutions was shaken. The news media relayed all the great social and political questions of the day and, amid the clash and clamor, came to be questioned themselves. Such timely issues as objectivity and the use of anonymous sources have been treated in journalism films, though symbolically and with a covert purpose. Beneath their surface realism, the films work to reconcile the turbulent present with traditional beliefs, to melt it into myth.

Hollywood felt the powerful aftershocks of the cultural upheavals of the sixties and seventies. Whatever remained of the studio system as it operated in the thirties and forties, the so-called "golden age of Hollywood," collapsed. Studios had no distinctive style, no stable of contract players, no circuit of theaters. The dream factories became part of conglomerates like Gulf and Western (Paramount) and TransAmerica (United Artists). MGM, which once boasted "more stars than in heaven," ceased film production and auctioned off its props and wardrobes, including Judy Garland's ruby slippers from *The Wizard of Oz.* Today the studios are primarily financiers and distributors, interested only in bankable projects and profit margins.[5] "The deal, that's all this business is about," a producer at Twentieth Century—Fox told John Gregory Dunne. "Who's available, when can you get him, start date, stop date, percentages."[6]

In 1985, and again in 1986, independent filmmakers made more pictures than the studios. But the demise of the studio system in the sixties and seventies didn't mean the end of traditional genres. As Leonard Quart and Albert Auster wrote, "Genre films with their well-defined characters, actions and iconography still resonated with

American audiences."[7] It is most useful to approach the journalism film as three sub-genres, a sort of triptych, with each panel revealing a different facet of the screen image of the journalist. The first shows a war correspondent losing his bearings in an orphan country of bombed-out buildings and mass graves; the second, a reporter destroying innocent lives while madly chasing scoops; and the last, an investigative journalist unraveling a far-reaching conspiracy. Taken together, the sub-genres represent the public's complex, often contradictory expectations of the press.

"A man watches a movie," Robert Warshow said, "and the critic must acknowledge that he is that man."[8] My analyses and ironic asides are rooted in who I am, but who I am comes as a surprise sometimes even to me. Alone with my notes and obscure obsessions, I have recorded what I saw in the bright shadows on the screen, my best version of the truth. And how good is that? I remember a strange thing that used to happen to me after a long, hectic night on the news desk. I would go home, fall into an uneasy sleep, and dream in headlines. My overcharged brain couldn't stop writing 1–30–3's and 2–48–2's and 6–72–1's. I would be wrestling with a tight count when the sun would wake me. Immediately, I would forget the headlines I had dreamed. The popular conception of journalists is similarly elusive, a phantom rider, a ghost. I have gone into the dark to seek it.

## Notes

1. Charles Maland, "*Dr. Strangelove* (1964): Nightmare Comedy and the Ideology of Liberal Consensus," in *Hollywood As Historian: American Film in a Cultural Context,* ed. by Peter C. Rollins (Lexington, Ky.: University of Kentucky Press, 1983), p. 208.

2. Among the more egregious examples are George N. Fenin and William K Everson, *The Western: From Silents to the Seventies* (New York: Grossman, 1973); Jon Tuska, *The Detective in*

*Hollywood* (Garden City, N.Y.: Doubleday, 1978); and Wiley Lee Umphlett, *The Movies Go to College: Hollywood and the World of College-Life Film* (Cranbury, N.J.: Associated University Press, 1984).

3. Thomas Schatz, *Hollywood Genres: Formulas, Filmmaking, and the Studio System* (New York: Random House, 1981), p. 226.

4. Vivian Sobchack, "Genre Film: Myth, Ritual, and Sociodrama," in *Film/Culture: Explorations of Cinema in its Social Context,* ed. by Sari Thomas (Metuchen, N.J.: Scarecrow Press, 1982), p. 148.

5. Lester D. Friedman, *Hollywood's Image of the Jew* (New York: Frederick Ungar, 1982), pp. 176–77; Leonard Quart and Albert Auster, *American Film and Society Since 1945* (New York: Praeger, 1984), pp. 75, 104–05.

6. John Gregory Dunne, *The Studio* (New York: Farrar, Straus & Giroux, 1969), p. 100.

7. Quart and Auster, *American Film,* p. 105.

8. Robert Warshow, *The Immediate Experience* (New York: Atheneum, 1975), p. 27.

# SHARED FICTIONS

> It is a poor idea of fantasy which takes it to be a world apart from reality....—Stanley Cavell, *The World Viewed*

WHEN TOM WOLFE TOOK his first newspaper job in 1957, he thought of journalism as he had seen it portrayed on the screen. After five long years within the ivy-covered, claustrophobic confines of Yale, where he earned a Ph.D. in American Studies, Wolfe had an uncontrollable craving for something wildly different, something lurid and free-wheeling. He dreamed of "Drunken reporters out on the ledge of the *News* peeing into the Chicago River at dawn... Nights down at the saloon listening to 'Back of the Yards' by a baritone who was only a lonely blind bulldyke with lumps of milk glass for eyes...Nights down at the detective bureau." He wanted, as he said, "the whole movie, nothing left out...."[1]

It is a sign of the professional pretensions of journalists today that their brassy movie cousins alarm rather than enthrall them. The press, on reaching middle age, has grown more conservative and begun to fret about its public image. Pondering the causes of the credibility crisis that struck journalism with the force of an A-bomb in the early 1980s, Walker Lundy, executive editor of the *Tallahassee* (Fla.) *Democrat,* wrote: "Over the years, we've done a decent job of reporting on everyone's business but our own. Most people get their impressions of us from Hollywood."[2] Clearly, Lundy didn't think that Hollywood was doing the press any favors by filling the vacuum. In September 1986 the Los Angeles chapter of the Society of Professional Journalists founded Operation Watchdog, aimed at "leading creative people in the right direction" when portraying journalists on film. With unconscious irony, the pressure group aimed as well at "increasing public appreciation of the First Amendment."[3]

But nothing the self-appointed censors can do or say is likely to lessen the attraction of journalism as a subject for movies. Writer-director Sam Fuller, who was a police reporter on the old *New York Evening Journal,* claimed that the newspaperman and filmmaker are indissolubly linked by temperament and technique, "sharing bloodstained scissors, glue, proofs, cement, splicer, work print…." "Page One and the Screen are bedmates," he said. The casting of a combat photographer as the main character in both *Under Fire* (1983) and *Salvador* (1986)—the viewfinder framing a protagonist slowly waking up to how much of life and death a viewfinder can't contain—would seem to justify Fuller's hyperbole that the journalist and movie director "spill blood on the same emotional battlefield of what is fit to print and what is fit to film."[4]

Moviegoers, too, have closely identified with the journalist, or at least the supercharged vision of the journalist invented for the screen. If they hadn't, the newspaper film wouldn't have endured since the days of pantomime and title cards. There were silent pictures about reporters catching criminals (*The Passionate Pilgrim,* 1921, and *Midnight Secrets,* 1924); reporters exposing the decadence of high society (*Salome of the Tenements,* 1925); and reporters breaking political machines (*What a Night,* 1928).[5]

Various scholars have attempted to explain the lasting appeal of the newspaper film. "As an institution which daily informs our perception of the world," Thomas H. Zynda of the University of Iowa suggested, "the press is… salient in the consciousness of the audience. At the same time, the audience lacks concrete knowledge about it as an institution, about how exactly it operates and what life in it is like. The press is hence clothed with an aura of importance and some mystery that lends it well to the dramatic requirements of popular art."[6] Mindful of the countless films in which the reporter plays detective, John Belton of Columbia University said: "The audience is trying to solve whatever mystery there is, and the reporter is our agent. He has the power to see things and make sense out of them. We identify with him as an ideal ego because he can do more than we can." William Everson of New York University attributed to the reporter "the individualism, excitement and get-up-and-go of the old-time cowboy. He's very much on his own and willing to take on the mob to win a point."[7]

These explanations are all right as far as they go, but they don't go far enough. They overlook the darker facets of the movie image of the journalist. Up on the screen, individualism often slips over the line into self-seeking, and excitement into irresponsibility. Hollywood has given us reporters corrupted by cynicism, ambition, and drink, careless of others' lives and reputations, and ever reluctant to let the truth stand in the way of a good story. After seeing ten newspaper films made between 1931 and 1974, Nora Sayre, critic for the *New York Times,* remarked, "Small wonder that many moviegoers don't love or trust newspaper people; from the first film production of 'The Front Page' to the latest, over 30 years of movies have stated that reporters blithely invent the news while ignoring what really happened, and that the newsroom is a giant nursery seething with infantile beings."[8]

The contradictory portrayal of the journalist as part knight-errant, part scoundrel, and part wise guy has its roots in popular literature.[9] In the 1890s, a new class of fiction emerged in America that took, for better or worse, the reporter for its hero. By the early 1930s, when "talkies" appropriated the character, he had already hardened into a distinct type. He was an exaggerated reflection of his creators, newspapermen and former newspapermen with ambivalent feelings about what journalism had done for them and to them.

Between 1890 and 1930, as the population of cities swelled with successive waves of record immigration, and as mechanical breakthroughs made larger and faster press runs possible, newspapers gathered a mass audience. Circulation and revenues soared to undreamed-of heights, and the reporter could boast that he was "a citizen of no mean state."[10] The period saw journalism assume some of the trappings of a profession. Press clubs sprang up, trade journals appeared, and the movement for college instruction in journalism got seriously under way.

But the spectacular growth in the wealth and power of the press also was accompanied by a chorus of abuse, particularly from the educated classes. They complained that the mass-circulation dailies, with big, black headlines screaming of murder, misfortune, and madness, pandered to the semiliterate and poisoned the atmosphere of American life. The reporter acted as if he were indifferent to the criticism, even proud of his ability to outrage the custodians of official culture. Beneath his apparent jauntiness, however, he longed for public acknowledgment that his was an important new calling. The failure to receive it cut deeply into his self-image as a man to be envied and respected. Theodore Dreiser, who had been a reporter in the 1890s, said that the "newspaper profession, the reporting end of it, was the roughest, most degrading, most disheartening of any.... Only the poor and the outcasts seemed to stand in awe of us, and not even those at times."[11]

The trauma of social rejection threw an indelible shadow over newspaper fiction. Novel after now-forgotten novel defines journalism, in the words of one of them, as a "strange world where brilliant young men turn out to be sad old men."[12] An alcoholic, prematurely aged reporter in David Graham Phillips' *The Great God Success* (1901) says: "Journalism is not a career. It is either a school or a cemetery. A man may use it as a stepping-stone to something else. But if he sticks to it, he finds himself dead and done for to all intents and purposes before he's buried."[13] In Henry Justin Smith's *Deadlines* (1923), the city editor warns an innocent cub: "Business'll kill you if you keep on. Look at me, hauled out of bed at five every morning; rush to my desk, stay there till the last dog's hung. Fight, fight, fight, all the time. Fight with the staff, with the readers of the paper, with the town.... Get a quieter job.... Nothing in this boiler-shop grind...."[14] A broken-down reporter in Ben Ames Williams' *Splendor* (1927) echoes: "There's no future for a man in the newspaper business. Nothing but a lot of work and a sanitarium when your nerves play out. Late hours, long hours, dull scratching at things."[15]

Even the crusading journalist, the most glamorous figure in the literary portrait gallery of newspapermen, is streaked with darkness and moral decay. Whether he tangles with vigilantes (Booth Tarkington's *The Gentleman from Indiana,* 1899), Wall Street swindlers (Charles Agnew Maclean's *The Mainspring,* 1912), or patent-medicine charlatans (Samuel Hopkins Adams' *The Clarion,* 1914), he typically has no more conscience than the wrongdoers he exposes. His reporting may benefit the public and further the ends of justice in the long run, but his first loyalty is to scoops and circulation. "[N]ow and then when I stumble on a fact which is news, I print it," the hardboiled hero of John C. Mellet's *Ink* (1930) explains. "If readers are surprised, or horrified, or startled into action, that is all right with me. If not, all right too. I'm only interested in printing things that will interest them...."[16] Anxious to beat the competition, a reporter will do almost anything short of murder to score an exclusive. The title character of Olin L. Lyman's *Micky* (1905) chloroforms a political boss, and while the "Napoleon of graft" lies knocked out on the floor, steals incriminating documents from his pocket.[17] An ideal motto for the sensationmongers in crusader's armor is supplied by the managing editor of the *San Francisco News* in Miriam Michelson's *A Yellow Journalist* (also 1905): "A newspaper is a business property, not a school of ethics."[18]

Standing over the reporters and editors, lashing them to frenzies of sensationalism, are greedy, hypocritical publishers. Adams wrote in *Success* (1921), the last and bleakest of his three newspaper novels, that "The men who go to the top in journalism...come through with a contempt for the public which they serve, compared to which the contempt of the public for the newspaper is as skim milk to corrosive sublimate."[19] David Holman, the Hearst-like press baron in William Richard Hereford's *The Demagog* (1909), may lead the pack in cynicism. He claims in editorials to speak for "the People, the Real People, the majority who have been dumb so long," but refers in private to what his yellow journals publish as "pabulum for the masses."[20] He pretends concern for the lot of the factory worker and immigrant merely to better manipulate them for his own profit and glory.

The amoral publisher later surfaced in films like *Five-Star Final* (1931), *Nothing Sacred* (1937), *Mr. Deeds Goes to Town* (1940), and *Park Row* (1952), spouting smarmy journalistic platitudes to dignify circulation stunts or camouflage unholy political ambitions. Orson Welles' *Citizen Kane* (1940), for all its technical genius, was as firmly bound to the stereotype of the egomaniacal newspaper tycoon as dozens of lesser films ("People will think what I tell them to think," Kane declares at one point). Nor does the ominous figure give any sign of vanishing soon. He has been reincarnated as a TV executive obsessed with ratings in *Network* (1976) and *Wrong Is Right* (1982) and as a cold-blooded media consultant in *Power* (1986).

All of which is to say that newspaper films, and the newspaper plays from which some of the more famous films were adapted, owe their stock characters and situations to newspaper fiction. *Front Page Woman* (1935) indirectly acknowledged this. A cub (Bette Davis) arrives at a prison one night to cover her first execution. When a writer for a rival paper (George Brent) voices surprise that she would request such a gruesome assignment, she snaps: "Why not? I'm a reporter." He smiles pityingly at her. "No, you're not," he says. "You're just a sweet little kid whose family let her read too many newspaper novels."

Works of newspaper fiction occasionally achieved brief popularity. More than 50,000 copies of Richard Harding Davis' *Gallegher, A Newspaper Story* (1890) were sold, a considerable number for the time. Henry Sydnor Harrison's *Queed* (1911), Katharine Brush's *Young Man of Manhattan,* and Edna Ferber's *Cimarron* (both 1930) also became best sellers. But the genre as a whole never attracted the mass audience the newspaper film did. The movies took common literary clay and breathed new life into it. Brought to the big screen, the image of the journalist was magnified and put in noisy and anarchic motion. The characters and settings readers once had to piece together in their own imaginations were immediately and volubly present to moviegoers. The very titles of the early sound films—*It Happened One Night* (1934), *Murder Man* (1935), *Too Hot to Handle* (1938), *Scandal Sheet* (1939)—promised adventure and mystery and romance. As Pauline Kael said, "A newspaper picture meant a contemporary picture in an American setting . . . a tough modern talkie, not a tearjerker with sound."[21]

The Hollywood reporter of the 1930s and 1940s cursed his calling, yet clung to it. He wore a hat indoors, had a bottle of booze stashed in his bottom desk drawer, and insulted everyone he met. He could be shrewd, sardonic, and, if necessary (and sometimes even if unnecessary), ruthless. It was *The Front Page* (1931), directed by Lewis Milestone and based on Ben Hecht and Charles MacArthur's 1928 Broadway hit, that crystallized the screen persona of the newspaperman, much to the discredit of the press. "*The Front Page* and its progeny," Doug Fetherling wrote in his biography of Hecht, "have created healthy suspicions about journalism and its servants in the minds of millions of people who otherwise have no real knowledge of either."[22]

Most of the action takes place in the dingy press room of a criminal courts building (presumably in Chicago; the city is never identified in the film version), where a group of reporters is waiting to cover the hanging of cop-killer Earl Williams. They pass the time wisecracking, gargling with whisky, playing poker, and goading prostitute Mollie Molloy into jumping out the window. "Hard work, ain't it?" one of them says between yawns. When Williams escapes, and again when he is recaptured, they grab the phones, bawl to the rewrite men at the other end of the lines, "Get this!", and proceed to shamelessly embroider the facts. What they have instead of scruples is a rakish style, and in a mad, malevolent universe of bribes, frame-ups, and random gunfire, style almost seems a kind of courage.

Hecht helped originate—"instigate" might be a better word—not only the newspaper picture, but also the gangster film. Drawing on his experiences as a young crime reporter in Chicago, he wrote the Academy Award-winning scenario for director Josef von Sternberg's *Underworld* (1927), "the first gangster film with modern credentials."[23] Gangland's one-way rides, shootouts, and bombings were big news during Prohibition, and gangster movies borrowed freely from the headlines. After repeal in 1933, when the gangster was temporarily retired as a popular film hero, the reporter was a natural choice to inherit his spotted mantle.[24]

Like the gangster, the newspaperman was defined on the screen by brashness and cunning. Both were creatures of the city, peculiarly attuned to its fast pace, crowds, and opportunities to get ahead.[25] They reflected the American preference for action and accomplishment rather than ideology, and embodied the myth of the self-reliant individual who pits his nerves and resourcefulness against the suffocating norms of society.

When a journalist wearied of his rough-and-tumble life, he might talk of going into another line of work and starting a family, but something deep inside him continued to resist a change in his career and allegiances. Marriage represented the ultimate surrender to convention. "It makes a respectable citizen out of a man," a reporter in *The Front Page* says. No worse fate could possibly be imagined by the boys in the press room. A newspaperman was already married to his job, and gaining a divorce to remarry a "nice girl" was an extreme step, one likely to be regretted as soon as taken.

*The Front Page,* as Molly Haskell commented, was a love story (or a love-hate story) between demon editor Walter Burns and star reporter Hildy Johnson.[26] Burns was modeled on Walter Howey, the infamous city editor of the *Chicago Examiner,* for whom MacArthur had worked. Howey discouraged matrimony among his staff, cutting the salaries of those who sullied their affection for the paper with affection for their wives.[27] In the film, Burns does everything in his power to sabotage Hildy's wedding plans and call him back to his first love, the male world of crime reporting. It is unclear at the end whether Hildy will ever make good his escape, though it is very clear that he would be a "firehorse tied to a milk wagon" if he did.

Newspaper films still depict the average woman as a domesticator. Christine, the teacher girlfriend of the reporter hero of *The Mean Season* (1985), is a contemporary version of the schoolmarm in Westerns. She is the apostle of civilization and the whiny voice of conscience. The reporter has promised to quit his job and move with her to Colorado, far away from the sordidness of big-city journalism, but then gets caught up in covering a serial murderer. She keeps reminding him of the social and personal costs of his involvement with the story, and eventually he comes around to her moral views. His careless childhood days have ended.

Journalism was once an overwhelmingly masculine institution, offering women only the frills and fringes of newspaper work. In 1903 there were fewer than 300 regularly employed newspaperwomen in the United States.[28] Thirty-one years later, Stanley Walker, city editor of the *New York Herald Tribune,* said female journalists "are not yet out of the twilight zone." Most, he explained, "are shunted into special departments, where they do not have to deal with ... policemen, firemen, ambulances, gunmen, lawyers and politicians in the back room."[29] It wasn't until the women's rights movement quickened in the 1970s that female journalists finally began to escape the pink-collar ghettos.[30] Their rising professional status has translated into greater prominence on the screen. They now are entitled to display in films the same single-minded devotion to the job as their male colleagues.

In *The China Syndrome* (1979), Jane Fonda is a TV correspondent eager to make the jump from features to hard news. Her ambition pushes everything else out of her life. She gives and receives no intimacies. Her family consists of a pet turtle, her camera crew, and the disembodied voice of her mother on a telephone answering machine. She is a sort of nun, her passion consecrated to the jealous gods of journalism.

"After you have been a newspaper writer ...," reporter-turned-novelist Edna Ferber said, "you will always be a newspaper writer, at least by heart or by instinct, until you die."[31] The character played by Susan Sarandon in *Compromising Positions* (1985), a former newspaperwoman married to a Wall Street lawyer and living in expensive style in suburbia, neatly illustrates the point. When her Lothario of a dentist is murdered, her long-repressed reporter's instinct bursts forth. She investigates the crime over the outraged objections of her husband, who feels her slipping away into a world where he can't follow. Her compulsive interest in the case is a form of adultery. She jeopardizes marriage and motherhood to hunt down the killer. In modern journalism films, equality of the sexes means that male and female journalists are equally trapped in the cold, lonely straits of their professional identities.

It is a rare film today that honors journalists for their absolute commitment to their profession, or that celebrates their legendary disdain for legal niceties and ethical restraints. The newspapermen (and occasional newspaperwoman) who frantically chased stories in the films of the 1930s and 1940s entertained by cracking rude jokes about ethics and wearing their cynicism like a badge. Journalism films of the past 25 years, on the other hand, have resonated with a "new tone of seriousness that sometimes border[s] on righteousness."[32] Although the image of journalists has been darkened by moral ambiguity ever since emerging a century ago from second-rate novels, the journalist characters themselves have never been so conscious of the ambiguity as now. Whether catching crooks or covering wars, they are shown locked in existential dilemmas. They struggle with questions of truth and fiction, objectivity and subjectivity, compassion and distance.

Such films are part of the noisy debate over the nature and role of the press that broke out amid the social upheavals of the 1960s, and that hasn't appreciably quieted yet. From the long hot summers of rioting and looting to the "Summer of Love," from student strikes to air strikes, from the coronation of political celebrities to assassinations and assassination attempts, from ban-the-Bomb marches to "Support Our Boys in Vietnam" rallies, journalists often were blamed for trends and events they only reported.

The impulse to "kill the messenger" for the bad tidings he brought was seen in the public reaction to the clashes between antiwar protesters and police at the 1968 Democratic National Convention in Chicago. Lawyer Daniel Walker investigated the disorders for the National Commission on the Causes and Prevention of Violence. The Walker Report labeled what happened "a police riot" in which journalists, generally peaceful protesters, and innocent bystanders were tear-gassed and clubbed. It said the terror in the streets was worse than the media described. But the public thought differently; they believed that the TV networks paid too much attention to the protesters. A majority of Americans supported the actions of the police, and the press left Chicago with its reputation tarnished.[33]

Richard Nixon, who never forgave reporters for not trusting or adoring him as they had his political rival, John Kennedy, exploited and expanded public suspicion of the press after becoming president in 1968. Former White House speechwriter William Safire said Nixon stressed again and again, "The press is the enemy." In the fall of 1969 Nixon's animus reached epic proportions when the press pummeled his appointment of Clement F. Haynsworth, Jr. to the Supreme Court, questioned his hard line on Vietnam, and ridiculed his appeal to "the great Silent Majority of my fellow Americans." He struck back at his tormentors in a November 13 speech given by Vice President Spiro Agnew in Des Moines, Iowa. Nixon went over the speech line by line with its author, Pat Buchanan, toughened it in a couple of places, and then chortled, "This really flicks the scab off, doesn't it?" The speech raked the "dozen anchormen, commentators, and executive producers [who]... decide what forty to fifty million Americans will learn of the day's events in the nation and in the world... read the same newspapers... draw their political and social views from the same sources... talk constantly to one another, thereby providing artificial reinforcement to their shared viewpoint."[34]

For the next two and a half years, Nixon kept up his campaign of intimidation against the press, with—from his perspective—encouraging results. When Bob Woodward and Carl Bernstein, young *Washington Post* reporters, began to peel back the layers of the Watergate scandal in the summer of 1972, they got very little help from their colleagues. Agnew's speech, echoed repeatedly by Nixon and his aides, had put the press on the defensive. "Newspapers and magazines were beset by irresolution and self-doubt," J. Anthony Lukas recalled, "half-believing that they were part of some coterie of effete Eastern intellectuals out to get the President."[35] A few weeks before the Nixon landslide in the 1972 presidential election, a Gallup poll found that 48 percent of Americans had never even heard of Watergate.[36] Until grand jury and congressional investigations made the story credible, the press shied away from it. Reporters tried to compensate for their late start by their enthusiastic attendance at the kill. In August 1974 Nixon resigned rather than face impeachment. Journalistic folklore credited "Woodstein," as the *Post*'s reporting team came to be known, and other crusaders of the press with driving him from the White House.

Justifiably or not, Watergate restored some of the prestige and glamor the press had lost in the sixties. In the aftermath of the scandal, enrollments in journalism schools shot up. Meanwhile, young reporters, eager for the celebrity of Woodstein, tended to take an adversary stance toward government, to see a potential Watergate in almost every story. But the apotheosis of the press was short-lived. Investigative reporters may regularly win prizes, but they rarely win friends. As Walker Lundy said, "A good, aggressive newspaper is often not a very likable institution. ...Eventually, we get around to angering most people and organizations in town."[37] The press-bashing that had marked the Nixon era returned with a vengeance. Journalists were accused of being too liberal, too negative, too sensational, too remote.

The press was convalescent for the first six years of the Reagan administration, chronically unable or unwilling to exert itself. Then came the revelation that contrary to stated policy, and possibly federal law, the administration had sold weapons to Iran and had diverted the profits to rebels in Nicaragua. Visions of another Watergate, as well as a mistaken sense that President Reagan's popularity was waning, brought the press back to life. After the story—dubbed "Irangate"—leaked in November 1986, Reagan told *Time* magazine, "I've never seen the sharks circling like now with blood in the water."[38] Many Americans must have agreed. Two months into the scandal, the credibility of the press had plunged 17 points, according to a Times Mirror/Gallup poll.[39] A widely publicized remark by Ben Bradlee, executive editor of the *Washington Post,* that he "hadn't had so much fun since Watergate," only served to reinforce the impression that journalists were drunk on blood.[40]

Wherever human misery is at its worst, there you will find the press in force—shouting questions and sticking microphones and cameras in the faces of the victims. Reporters come off in these wild encounters as unfeeling, even ghoulish. An incident in January 1987 showed the press in a particularly negative light. At a news conference called to announce his resignation, Pennsylvania Treasurer R. Budd Dwyer pulled out a revolver, stuck it in his mouth, and fired. WPVI-TV in Philadelphia ran the suicide in gruesome, unedited color. Supposedly responsible papers published a series of four photographs of the shooting. Gene Roberts, executive editor of the *Philadelphia Inquirer,* reasoned, "They had blood flying and all that on a Philadelphia television station this morning, so I don't think we're going to be shocking any of our readers."[41] And journalists wonder why the public detests them?

Journalists are given to making fine declarations about freedom of the press and the public's right to know, but their actions undercut their soaring rhetoric. Avowals of knight-errantry sound doubly strange coming from employees of the third-largest industry in the United States and one of the ten most profitable.[42] Dazzled by the millions of dollars to be made, national and multinational corporations swept across the media landscape in the period 1965–80 like a Mongol horde, conquering and sacking. "What has changed," wrote James Boylan of the University of Massachusetts at Amherst, "is that... almost every major newspaper is now part of a larger corporate structure... a bureaucracy in a society in which bureaucracies are the major institution."[43] Twenty corporations control more than half the 61 million papers sold every day, and the capitalistic ethos dictates that the companies place their loyalty to stockholders above their loyalty to readers.[44] The result has been a growing perception that the greatest threat to the quality and diversity of the press may be the press itself.

Compounding the "image problem" of journalists is the feeling that they care little about getting their facts straight. "Our concern for accuracy," Lundy conceded, "often amounts to writing that mother up and shoving it in the paper pronto."[45] In 1982 Larry Beaupre, managing editor of the *Rochester* (N.Y.) *Times-Union*, examined a representative sample of 36 U.S. and Canadian papers for the American Press Institute. He found "a lot of sloppy and imprecise writing that raised doubts about the authenticity or source of the information in the story." He also found that corrections were sometimes buried in the back of a paper with the truss ads.[46]

The public's ugliest suspicions about the press seemed to be confirmed in 1981 by an outbreak of plagiarism and fakery. *Washington Post* reporter Janet Cooke was forced to return a Pulitzer Prize after admitting that she had fabricated "Jimmy's World," a profile of an 8-year-old heroin addict. A month later, Michael Daly of the *New York Daily News* acknowledged that he had invented key details in an interview with a British soldier who, he had alleged, had shot a teenager in Northern Ireland. Even the august *New York Times* was hit by fraud when its Sunday magazine published an article by freelancer Christopher Jones about a journey through Khmer Rouge-held areas of Cambodia. Actually, Jones hadn't stirred from his home in Spain and had plagiarized the final paragraph of his piece from André Malraux's 1923 novel, *La Voie Royale*. He was quickly exposed, and Cooke and Daly were fired, but the damage they did to the credibility of all journalists was substantial and irreparable.

It is clear from the huge sums awarded by juries in

recent libel trials that confidence in the press is precarious. "This is a bad decade for the news media in the courtroom," Washington libel lawyer Bruce Sanford said.[47] The Libel Defense Resource Center, in a study of 47 libel cases that reached juries from 1980–82, reported that the press lost 42 of them. In more than half the cases, judgments exceeded $100,000, and several were in the million-dollar-plus category.[48] Although most of the "megaverdicts" are reduced or overturned on appeal, Eugene Patterson, editor of the *St. Petersburg* (Fla.) *Times,* lamented: "Juries are the American people. They want to punish us."[49]

Desperate for some sign that they have been reprieved, journalists have grown preoccupied with their standing in opinion polls. But despite this obsession, they have been curiously unable to defuse public hostility toward the press. The reason may be that they can't bring themselves to face its ultimate causes. They flee difficult questions of policy and ethics that must be addressed before they can staunch the hemorrhaging of their credibility. It is less threatening and disruptive to journalistic routine for them to see the controversy over press performance as a problem in public relations rather than as a crisis in professional values. And so, overlooking displays of their own arrogance and incompetence, they commonly blame their fallen estate on the arrogance and incompetence of others: politicians, the courts, conservatives, and, of course, Hollywood.

"[M]any news people," Nora Sayre said, "feel that pictures have maligned them as badly as other pictures have caricatured priests and psychiatrists."[50] Ironically, the portrayal that has discomforted journalists was largely created by their former colleagues. With the introduction of sound films, newspaper folk swarmed to Hollywood to try their hands at screenwriting. The director Broaca in F. Scott Fitzgerald's *The Last Tycoon* (1941) could remember the days "when writers were gag-men or eager and ashamed young reporters full of whisky. . . ."[51] From newspaper hack to Hollywood hack was a short step. Journalists were "used to regarding their work not as deathless prose, but as stories written to order for the market. . . ."[52] They were well prepared to become the scenarists of the talkies. "On a newspaper you get kicked around," explained $1,000-a-day screenwriter Ben Hecht. "You learn the hard way. You gotta sit down and write it, ready or not. That's how I learned to write fast. I c'n write a novel in four weeks. A screenplay in two. Just pound it out and let the poetry take care of itself."[53]

Other screenwriters who served an apprenticeship in journalism included Rian James (*Love Is A Racket,* 1932), Allen Rivkin (*Is My Face Red,* 1932), Roy Chanslor (*Hi, Nellie,* 1934, and *Front Page Woman*), Lamar Trotti (*Life Begins at Forty,* 1935), Claude Binyon (*The Gilded Lily* and *The Bride Comes Home,* both 1935), Dalton Trumbo (*Road Gang,* 1936), Art Arthur (*Love and Hisses,* 1938, and *Everything Happens at Night,* 1939), Herman J. Mankiewicz (*Citizen Kane*), Harry Kurnitz (*Shadow of the Thin Man,* 1941), and Sam Fuller (*Confirm or Deny,* 1941). A list of newspapermen turned screenwriters fills almost two pages of Alex Barris' *Stop the Presses!*[54] In the newspaper pictures they wrote and, in some cases, also directed, the former reporters and editors were commenting on a milieu they knew intimately. Deac Rossell, film coordinator at Boston's Museum of Fine Arts, described their movies as "fondly bitter reminiscences of lost youth by men graduated from the world of newswriting to screenwriting."[55]

Contemporary journalism films carry on the tradition. The script of *Between the Lines* (1977), a movie about life on an alternative newspaper in Boston, was written by Fred Barron, an alumnus of the *Boston Phoenix* and *The Real Paper.* Kurt Ludetke was executive editor of the *Detroit Free Press* before he wrote *Absence of Malice* (1981). Several of the films have been adapted from books or articles by journalists. *The Mean Season* was based on the novel, *In the Heat of the Summer* (1982) by John Katzenbach, who covered police and courts for the *Miami Herald,* and *The Killing Fields* (1984) on the magazine story, "The Death and Life of Dith Pran" by Sydney Schanberg, who reported the fall of Cambodia to the Khmer Rouge for the *New York Times.*

Yet we would be wrong to think that a journalism film

is realistic simply because it was written by a former newspaperman. According to the latest national survey, the typical American journalist is a politically moderate, 32-year-old, college-educated, married, white male Protestant earning $19,000 a year.[56] Not exactly the stuff dreams—or movies—are made of.

Hollywood offers entertainment and escape, not reality; seeks the biggest possible audience and profits, not truth. Money has always been, in screenwriter William Goldman's phrase, "the essential glue that binds the movie powers to each other."[57] But the talk of money dominates the film industry as never before. The average cost of a movie is $15 million and still soaring, propelled in part by stars' salaries (in 1986 Sylvester Stallone earned $12 million—a picture).[58] Because of the high stakes involved, studios are increasingly reluctant to stray too far from proven formulas. And from the perspective of the bottom line, the only perspective that seems to count, the strategy has worked. Five of the top ten moneymaking films of 1985 were sequels.[59] As anthropologist Hortense Powdermaker said in *Hollywood the Dream Factory:* "[I]f phoniness brings in money easily, why bother about details of honesty?"[60]

Journalism films reflect each other more than the realities of daily journalism. "The subject matter of any film story," Thomas Schatz pointed out, "is derived from certain 'real-world' characters, conflicts, settings, and so on. But once the story is repeated and refined into a formula, its basis in experience gradually gives way to its own internal logic."[61] A newsroom may look real on the screen, with computer terminals and dirty coffee cups on the desks and a background chorus of frantically ringing phones, but what occurs within the setting is an allegory, a fable. Newspaper life must be stylized and simplified to conform to the expectations of the audience and the rules of the genre. "This story is laid in a mythical kingdom," the opening title card of *The Front Page* announces, fair warning that despite the surface realism, we are about to cross the threshold of a fantasy.

*All the President's Men* (1976), adapted from the book by Carl Bernstein and Bob Woodward, provides an especially vivid example of the newsroom as mythic space, "space that," Richard Slotkin wrote, "has been coded for meaning, made to signify and symbolize."[62] Director Alan Pakula had a facsimile of the *Washington Post* newsroom built in Burbank, Calif., for $200,000. Two hundred desks were bought, identical to those at the *Post*, and 270 cartons of trash from the newspaper's wastebaskets were flown in.[63] But expensive props are no guarantee of authenticity, and the film that purports to tell the true story of the Watergate cover-up is very nearly a ritual drama. Interior shots of the newsroom are always brightly lit, in symbolic contrast with the shadowy streets of official Washington. The characters are transparent—ambitious kid reporter, gruff veteran editor, furtive source—and familiar from other films. One scene, where Bernstein outsmarts a secretary to get in to see her boss, is completely fictional.[64] The makers of *All the President's Men* just couldn't resist the temptation to "Hollywood it up."[65]

Although usually quick to challenge the validity of films about the press, journalists reveled in the exaggerations of this picture. Here, at last, was a movie that met their heroic image of themselves, that accorded with the legends of their profession. "Men do not have with myth a relationship based on truth but on use . . . ," Roland Barthes said.[66] Journalists are no different from other people in believing a film if it fits the way they feel.

A primary—perhaps *the* primary—function of popular art is to find metaphorical solutions to real problems.[67] Robert Warshow noted that movies "seem to have an almost unlimited power to absorb and transform the discordant elements of our fragmented culture."[68] Two closely related conflicts underlie the narrative patterns of the journalism film genre, one between the journalist and his job, the other between the institution of the press and the well-ordered community. How the films express and resolve these conflicts are clues to the myths we live by, our shared and necessary fictions. Sometimes within a single film, but more spectacularly within the genre as a whole, the journalist promotes both darkness and light, cruelty and justice, individualism and social integration. His ambiguous identity bears the marks of the audience's own contradictory values and attitudes. He is a gate in the complex circuitry of a cultural dream.

"The impact of movies," Stanley Cavell wrote, "is too massive... to speak politely of involvement."[69] Meaning takes place in us, the viewers, awake in the dark and dreaming with eyes wide open. Our need to feel in control of events, or to know why we don't, informs our reactions. Movies offer streamlined visions of the life we lead, wish to lead, ought to lead.[70] Nothing prevents them from becoming a "perpetual alibi" for our frailties and follies.[71] We appeal to the heroes and villains of film in negotiating the world beyond the walls of shopping mall cinemas. John Gregory Dunne, journalist, novelist, and screenwriter, admitted: "It is difficult to banish the notion of one's own life situations as a scenario, appropriately scored.... Few situations fail to evoke a cinematic response; in matters of principle we play *High Noon,* in renunciation scenes *Casablanca.*"[72] Our memory holds a jumbled collection of images from movies, faces and settings and bits of action that give us our fix on reality.

We remember Randall, the managing editor of a slimy tabloid in *Five-Star Final,* compulsively washing his hands, as if soap and water could erase his shame and guilt. We remember another managing editor, played by Humphrey Bogart in *Deadline U.S.A.* (1951), answering the threats of a mobster with the thunder of the presses. We remember John Finley Horton, the investigative reporter in *Black Like Me* (1960), sitting on his bed in a run-down boardinghouse, pouring into a notebook his traumatic, firsthand experiences of racism in the Deep South. We remember Megan Carter, the ethically bewildered reporter in *Absence of Malice,* saying with a quaver in her voice: "I keep thinking there must be some rules to tell me what to do now. Maybe there aren't.... No rules, just me." We remember Boyle, the war photographer in *Salvador,* making his dreadful way with his camera across a slope of flyblown corpses. Long after the lights have come up and the screen has gone blank, we still remember and, in remembering, possess the world.

## *Notes*

1. Tom Wolfe, "The New Journalism," in *The New Journalism,* ed. by Tom Wolfe and E.W. Johnson (New York: Harper & Row, 1970), p. 3.

2. Walker Lundy, "Why do readers mistrust the press?" *Bulletin of the American Society of Newspaper Editors,* March 1982, p. 5.

3. "SPJ, SDX to watch journalist portrayals," *Editor and Publisher,* September 13, 1986, p. 49.

4. Sam Fuller, "News That's Fit to Film," *American Film* I:1 (October 1975): 20.

5. Deac Rossell, "Hollywood and the Newsroom," *American Film* I:1 (October 1975): 15.

6. Thomas H. Zynda, "The Hollywood Version: Movie Portrayals of the Press," *Journalism History* 6:1 (Spring 1979): 23.

7. Jane Gross, "Movies and the Press Are an Enduring Romance," *New York Times,* 2 June 1985, sec. 2, pp. 1, 19.

8. Nora Sayre, "Falling Prey to Parodies of the Press," January 1, 1975, *New York Times Encyclopedia of Film* (New York: Times Books, 1984), unpaged.

9. For a fuller discussion of the origins, themes, and implications of newspaper novels, see the author's *Acquainted With the Night: The Image of Journalists in American Fiction, 1890–1930* (Metuchen, N.J.: Scarecrow Press, 1986).

10. Quoted in Allen Churchill, *Park Row* (New York: Rinehart, 1958), p. 224.

11. Theodore Dreiser, "Out of My Newspaper Days," *Bookman,* vol. LIV, September 1921–February 1922, p. 429.

12. Malcolm Ross, *Penny Dreadful* (New York: Coward-McCann, 1929), p. 62.

13. David Graham Phillips, *The Great God Success* (New York: Grosset & Dunlap, 1901; reprint ed., Ridgewood, N.J.: Gregg Press, 1967), p. 11.

14. Henry Justin Smith, *Deadlines* (Chicago: Covici-McGee, 1923), p. 193.

15. Ben Ames Williams, *Splendor* (New York: Dutton, 1927), p. 205.

16. John C. Mellett, *Ink* (Indianapolis: Bobbs-Merrill, 1930), p. 146.

17. Olin L. Lyman, *Micky* (Boston: Richard G. Badger, 1905), p. 182.

18. Miriam Michelson, *A Yellow Journalist* (New York: Appleton, 1905), p. 176.

19. Samuel Hopkins Adams, *Success* (Boston: Houghton Mifflin, 1921), p. 282. The two other novels are *Common Cause* (1919) and the already mentioned *The Clarion.*

20. William Richard Hereford, *The Demagog* (New York: Henry Holt, 1909), p. 162.

21. Pauline Kael, *The Citizen Kane Book* (Boston: Little, Brown, 1971), p. 20.

22. Doug Fetherling, *The Five Lives of Ben Hecht* (Canada: Lester and Orpen, 1977), p. 68.

23. Carlos Clarens, *Crimes Movies: From Griffith to The Godfather and Beyond* (New York: Norton, 1981), p. 31.

24. *Ibid.*, pp. 102–03.

25. Rossell, "Hollywood and the Newsroom," p. 16.

26. Molly Haskell, *From Reverence to Rape: The Treatment of Women in the Movies* (New York: Rinehart and Winston, 1974), p. 134.

27. Fetherling, *Five Lives of Ben Hecht,* p. 75.

28. Edwin L. Shuman, *Practical Journalism* (New York: Appleton, 1903), p. 147.

29. Stanley Walker, *City Editor* (New York: Frederick A. Stokes, 1934), pp. 248, 251.

30. James Boylan, "Declarations of Independence," *Columbia Journalism Review,* 25th Anniversary Issue, November/December 1986, p. 39.

31. Edna Ferber, *Dawn O'Hara* (New York: Grosset & Dunlap, 1911), p. 47.

32. Gross, "Movies and the Press Are an Enduring Romance," p. 19.

33. Edwin Emery and Michael Emery, *The Press and America: An Interpretive History of the Mass Media,* 5th ed. (Englewood Cliffs, N.J.: Prentice-Hall, 1984), pp. 566–68.

34. J. Anthony Lukas, *Nightmare: The Underside of the Nixon Years* (New York: Bantam, 1977), pp. 366–67.

35. *Ibid.,* p. 373.

36. *Ibid.,* p. 374.

37. Lundy, "Why do readers mistrust the press?", p. 5.

38. "An Interview With the President," *Time,* December 8, 1986, p. 18.

39. "Dere Press Corps: Drop Dead," *Washington Journalism Review,* March 1987, p. 14.

40. Alex S. Jones, "Fairness Stressed By Nation's Media," *New York Times,* 5 December 1986, sec. 1, p. 13.

41. Quoted in Susan Fleming and Marc Gunther, "A question of ethics," *Poughkeepsie Journal,* 25 January 1987, p. 1D.

42. Ben H. Bagdikian, *Media Monopoly* (Boston: Beacon Press, 1983), p. 121.

43. Boylan, "Declarations of Independence," p. 45.

44. Bagdikian, *Media Monopoly,* p. 4.

45. Lundy, "Why do readers mistrust the press?" p. 5.

46. Larry Beaupre, "Content examples that lead to public distrust or skepticism," *Bulletin of the American Society of Newspaper Editors,* March 1982, pp. 20–21.

47. Quoted in Alvin P. Sanoff, "Behind Wave of Libel Suits Hitting Nation's Press," *U.S. News & World Report,* November 5, 1984, p. 53.

48. Maxwell McCombs and Laura Washington, "Opinion Surveys Conflict on Public Views of Press," in *Believing the News,* ed. by Donald Frye (St. Petersburg, Fla.: Poynter Institute for Media Studies, 1985), p. 183.

49. Quoted in William A. Henry, III, "Journalism Under Fire," *Time,* December 12, 1983, p. 77.

50. Sayre, "Falling Prey to Parodies of the Press," unpaged.

51. F. Scott Fitzgerald, *The Last Tycoon* (New York: Charles Scribner's Sons, 1941), p. 41.

52. Kael, *Citizen Kane Book,* pp. 12–13.

53. Quoted in Budd Schulberg, *Moving Pictures: Memories of a Hollywood Prince* (New York: Stein and Day, 1981), p. 400.

54. Alex Barris, *Stop the Presses!: The Newspaperman in American Films* (South Brunswick, N.J.: A.S. Barnes, 1976), pp. 19–20.

55. Rossell, "Hollywood and the Newsroom," p. 18.

56. Michael Schudson, "Who Are We?" *Columbia Journalism Review,* May/June 1986, pp. 59–61.

57. William Goldman, *Adventures in the Screen Trade* (New York: Warner Books, 1983), p. 71.

58. Bob Thomas, "Stars' salaries: The sky's the limit," *Poughkeepsie Journal,* 9 May 1986, p. 5D.

59. Richard Corliss, "Backing into the Future," *Time,* February 3, 1986, p. 63.

60. Hortense Powdermaker, *Hollywood the Dream Factory: An Anthropologist Looks at the Movie-Makers* (Boston: Little, Brown, 1950), p. 315.

61. Thomas Schatz, *Hollywood Genres: Formulas, Filmmaking, and the Studio System* (New York: Random House, 1981), p. 36.

62. Richard Slotkin, "Prologue to a Study of Myth and Genre in American Movies," in *Prospects: The Annual of American Cultural Studies,* vol. 9, ed. by Jack Salzman (Cambridge: Cambridge University Press, 1984), p. 424.

63. Seth Cagin and Philip Dray, *Hollywood Films of the Seventies* (New York: Harper & Row, 1984), p. 250.

64. Goldman, *Adventures in the Screen Trade,* p. 240.

65. *Ibid.*, p. 233.

66. Roland Barthes, *Mythologies,* trans. and ed. by Annette Levers (New York: Hill and Wang, 1972), p. 144.

67. Gerald Weales, *Canned Goods As Caviar: American Film Comedy of the 1930s* (Chicago: University of Chicago Press, 1985), p. 184.

68. Robert Warshow, *The Immediate Experience* (New York: Atheneum, 1975), p. 24.

69. Stanley Cavell, *The World Viewed: Reflections on the Ontology of Film,* enlarged ed. (Cambridge, Mass.: Harvard University Press, 1979), p. 154.

70. Jack Shadoian, *Dreams and Dead Ends: The American Gangster/Crime Film* (Cambridge, Mass.: MIT Press, 1979), p. x.

71. The phrase is Barthes', *Mythologies,* p. 123.

72. John Gregory Dunne, *The Studio* (New York: Farrar, Straus & Giroux, 1969), pp. 7–8.

# THE GHOSTS IN THE SHADOWS

All cultures are complex and all have their hidden savage sides waiting to erupt.—Sydney Schanberg, *The Death and Life of Dith Pran*

THE WORK OF WAR correspondents involves violence, danger, and drama, as they never tire of reminding us. Every war since the American Civil War has produced a new crop of memoirs in which reporters celebrate their own courage and cunning. They excitingly tell how, to meet a deadline or score a scoop, they braved gunfire, went for days without sleep and hot food, and outmaneuvered censors and competitors. Implicit in their fond reminiscences of hair-raising adventures far from the home office is the insane notion that war is somehow fun.

Beginning with Rudyard Kipling's *The Light That Failed* and Stephen Crane's *Active Service* (both 1899), Anglo-American fiction also has contributed its just share to the glamorization of war correspondence. Newspaper artist Dick Heldar, the hero of Kipling's novel, was supposedly following a natural masculine impulse when he joined a British column marching to the relief of General Gordon at Khartoum. "[T]here was a row, so I came," he simply states.[1] No more explanation was needed as long as men still believed that your education wasn't complete, your virility not yet proved, until you had been shot at. For Dick, war represented a flight from domesticity and responsibility, and his death in a dawn attack in the Sudan was meant to seem gloriously romantic, the ultimate escape from the workaday world.

*Active Service* unfolds against the opéra bouffe backdrop of the Greco-Turkish War of 1897, which Crane reported for William Randolph Hearst's sensational *New York Journal* and the *Westminster Gazette.* An American professor, his wife and daughter, and some students disappear while traveling in the Greek countryside, and it is up to correspondent Rufus Coleman to locate and rescue them. "He was on active service, an active service of the heart, and he felt that he was a strong man ready to conquer difficulties even as the olden heroes conquered difficulty," Crane wrote of his knight of the press table.[2] Dodging army patrols, artillery barrages, and angry peasants, Coleman leads the group to safety and is rewarded with a scoop and marriage to the professor's beautiful daughter.

Because the war correspondent was such a larger-than-life figure in memoirs and novels, as well as in plays like Richard Harding Davis' *The Galloper* (1906) and Bella and Samuel Spewack's *Clear All Wires* (1932), it was probably inevitable that Hollywood would discover the professional crisis-chaser by the early thirties. But it wasn't until *Foreign Correspondent* (1940), directed by Alfred Hitchcock and co-scripted (without credit) by the ubiquitous Ben Hecht, that he was finally and firmly established as a popular film hero.

According to the opening narrative titles, the film is dedicated to "those intrepid ones who went overseas to be the eyes and ears of America... To those clear-headed ones who now stand like recording angels among the dead and dying. The Foreign Correspondents." Despite the portentous introduction, the main character (played by Joel McCrea) is nothing more—or less—than a smart-alecky crime reporter pulled off beer-mob killings and race riots and turned loose in Europe on the eve of World War II. He is soon hot on the trail of a Nazi spy ring. "I don't know what's wrong with Europe," he says, "but I do know a story when I see one, and I'll keep after it until I get it or it gets me." This is no idle boast. He takes part in a wild car chase, climbs out a window onto a high, narrow ledge to elude a pair of assassins, and survives a plane crash at sea.

*Foreign Correspondent* is an entertaining mix of action,

comedy, romance—and patriotism. In the final scene, McCrea is broadcasting a special report to America from a London radio studio. An air raid erupts, and the studio goes dark. He throws away his script, grips the microphone, and with the crash of bombs for an obbligato, emotionally declares: "It's as if the lights were all out everywhere. Except in America. Keep those lights burning. Cover them with steel, ring them with guns, build a canopy of battleships and bombing planes around them. They're the only lights left." Then, as the closing credits roll, the familiar chords of "The Star-Spangled Banner" swell on the soundtrack.

The success of *Foreign Correspondent*—and the spread of the war—spawned a host of pale imitations, among them *Confirm or Deny* (1941), *Berlin Correspondent* (1942), *Passage to Marseille* (1944), and *Blood on the Sun* (1945).[3] Some 40 years later, the Vietnam War would inspire another wave of foreign correspondent films. But Vietnam wasn't World War II. As critic Michael Arlen pointed out, there were "no formal frontlines, no supportive illusions about a Holy War, no happy embrace of propaganda...."[4] It was a different world, a different war, and it called forth a different kind of celluloid correspondent.

He is less colorful, more coldly professional than his predecessors. McCrea's character wisecracked, "Give me an expense account, and I'll cover anything," and referred with typical exaggeration to his scoop as "the biggest story of the century." His modern counterpart often speaks of the responsibilities of journalism, growing particularly solemn about the need to be objective. But if some of the glamor and fun have gone out of foreign correspondence, none of the danger has. "You got to get close to get the truth," a combat photographer says in *Salvador* (1986). "Get too close, you die."

The correspondents in post-Vietnam films aren't only, or always primarily, after the truth. "If I can get some good combat shots for AP, I can make some money," says the main character in *Salvador,* a freelancer down on his luck. Driven by the powerful twin forces of professionalism and personal ambition, the correspondents have neither the time nor the interest to question the waste of war. They must lose themselves before they can find the real story, the story written in innocent blood.

"Which side are you on?" a left-wing Nicaraguan priest asks the hero of *Under Fire* (1983). "I don't take sides," the hero answers. "I'm a journalist." The priest studies him skeptically for a moment, then says, "Go home." He ignores the warning and is drawn with his colleagues into the vortex of a nightmare. One shell-shocked reporter exclaims, "Christ, what are we doing here?" "Here"—whether it is Central America in *Under Fire* and *Salvador* or Southeast Asia in *The Green Berets* (1968), *The Year of Living Dangerously* (1983), and *The Killing Fields* (1984)—is the place you would rather not know. It is the land of endless poverty and wounded dreams, of bomb craters and blowing black smoke, of torture rooms and assassination squads, of dismembered bodies and anonymous refugees, of child soldiers and helicopter gunships like flying dragons, of massacres and mass graves.

Little in the correspondents' previous experience has prepared them for their sudden descent into the underworld. Their orthodox brand of journalism can't cope with the rush of darkness. Stumbling through the valley of the shadow of death, they are tossed between their professional duty to report events objectively and their wakening impulse to intervene in disaster. They betray lovers, colleagues, assistants, and ideals as they struggle to reconcile their jobs with their consciences. Some emerge from the trial scarred but enlightened and add their voices to the anguished cry of the downtrodden for justice. "You've got to think of the people first," the protagonist of *Salvador* begs U.S. embassy officials. "In the name of human decency, something we Americans are supposed to believe in, you got to at least try to make something of a just society here." He has been allowed to return from the dead—"I heard you were killed," is the standard greeting he gets—that he might testify to the murderous rage of history.

Far-off, mysterious Vietnam is "the place where modern American history begins."[5] The Vietnam War was more heavily reported, analyzed, and debated in the press than any war before or since. At the time of the Tet offensive in late January 1968, between 600 and 700 correspondents were accredited to the Military Assistance Command, Vietnam. They were a strange assortment, including even feature writers for religious organs and gun magazines, and students from college newspapers. "There was no nation so impoverished, no hometown so humble," said Michael Herr, who covered the war for *Esquire,* "that it didn't get its man in for a quick feel at least once."[6]

In the last quarter of the nineteenth century, war correspondence had been the monopoly of a close-knit, largely British group of reporters, quasi-military men like William Howard Russell of the *Times* of London and Archibald Forbes of the *London Daily News.* Britain was engaged in a constant round of colonial wars, and every great London paper considered a war correspondent as necessary to its staff as an expert in sports, drama, or finance.[7] Wherever British soldiers went, there went the "specials" to telegraph back stories that would thrill the public.

The smoke-powder wars of Russell's time, which involved small numbers of troops on a limited front, were hardly wars at all by modern standards. A correspondent could see the whole battlefield through his field glasses, and the scenes that passed before his eyes contained elements of a splendid pageant. Swords and helmets flashed in the sun, and troops moved in serried ranks or formed squares to meet the enemy's charges. It was still possible to write of the romance of war when armistices were called to bury the dead, due courtesy was extended to the "other fellow," and battles conveniently ended with daylight.[8]

World War I brought revolutionary changes, both in combat and combat reporting. Dash and daring no longer won battles. Now troops leaped from trenches, advanced across no man's land toward an invisible enemy, and were mowed down in their thousands. The machine gun—which "would keep a stream of bullets in the air so dense that no one could walk upright in front of a machine-gunner's position without being hit"—had industrialized the act of killing.[9]

Bloody as the Great War was, cities and homes outside the combat zone had been spared. But World War II ushered in aerial bombing, and the distinction between civilians and soldiers vanished in the smoke and slaughter. CBS Radio correspondent William L. Shirer, accompanying Nazi troops on their invasions of Holland, Belgium, and France, was appalled at the random destructiveness of modern weapons. He could only exclaim in his diary: "What guns and bombs do to houses and people... to towns, cities, bridges, railroad stations and tracks and trains, to universities and ancient noble buildings, to enemy soldiers, trucks, tanks, and horses caught along the way!"[10] War had "ceased to be a gay thing," and so, too, had war correspondence.[11] In 1946 Herbert L. Matthews of the *New York Times,* who had first seen and fallen half in love with the face of war before the coming of long-range bombers, scorched-earth policies, and concentration camps, lamented that the "joys of battle and campaigning have been and are, in ever-increasing measure, dissolving into suffering.... "[12]

It was a lesson repeatedly illustrated by the Vietnam War. With its deep jungles, tangled rivers, and ghostly mountains, the country itself seemed as much the enemy as the North Vietnamese army and the elusive Viet Cong. The land was blasted and burned (Vietnam was more heavily bombed than either Germany or Japan had been in World War II), and its people were uprooted, terrorized, and murdered.[13] There was "a certain Alice in Wonderland character about the American effort."[14] Villages were destroyed in order to save them from communism.

Correspondents found it next to impossible to convey accurately what was happening, in part because they were handcuffed by journalistic conventions. "The problem," explained David Halberstam, who reported the war for the *New York Times,* "was trying to cover something every day as news when in fact the real key was that it was all derivative of the French Indo-China war, which is history. So you really should have had a third paragraph in each story which would have said, '... none of this means anything because we are in the same footsteps as the French and we are prisoners of their experience,' but given the rules of newspaper reporting you can't really do that."[15]

Other obstacles to full and honest coverage were posed by the American military machine. While there was little overt censorship in Vietnam, the military withheld or falsified information that might have undermined belief in the eventual success of U.S. policies. It employed a cosmetic language and phony statistics, like the infamous "body count," to disguise the futility of the struggle. The press corps cynically dubbed the daily military briefing in Saigon the "Five O'Clock Follies."[16]

Vietnam was proof of M.L. Stein's maxim that some commanders fear the press more than the enemy.[17] "[S]ooner or later," Michael Herr said, "all of us heard one version or another of 'My Marines are winning this war, and you people are losing it for us in your papers,' often spoken in an almost friendly way, but with the teeth shut tight behind the smiles. It was creepy," he added, "being despised in such casual, offhand ways."[18] The public was quite as suspicious as the military of the patriotism of the press and blamed correspondents who sent home stories that contradicted the official pronouncements of progress for dragging out the war.

On August 5, 1965, the CBS Evening News broadcast a film report on the destruction of the village of Cam Ne by Marines. "This is what the war in Vietnam is all about," correspondent Morley Safer said as he stood in front of the burning huts. "The Viet Cong were long gone... the action wounded three women, killed one baby, wounded one Marine and netted four old men as prisoners." The story caused a furor. Safer, who had tried to show the inhumanity of war, nearly lost his job.[19]

The repercussions were even greater when Harrison Salisbury of the *New York Times,* the first American journalist to visit Hanoi, filed a series of stories in December 1966 that punctured the inflated claims the Pentagon was making for the bombing of the enemy capital. He reported that U.S. planes had hit homes, hospitals, churches, and schools. Salisbury and the *Times* were criticized for publishing material favorable to North Vietnam. The credibility of the press suffered accordingly.[20]

Yet the plain fact is that the press in general was remarkably slow to question the methods and aims of the war. The few correspondents who did encountered resistance not only from the government and the public, but also from their colleagues in the news media. Halberstam, Neil Sheehan of United Press International, and Malcolm Brown of the Associated Press were among the earliest to challenge the wisdom of American policy. Their accounts of the spreading domestic opposition to the corrupt, U.S.-backed regime of South Vietnamese Premier Ngo Dinh Diem were hotly resented. In September 1963, *Time* magazine denounced Halberstam and company as propagandists plotting to overthrow Diem.[21]

Later the public would be loath to hear, and the mainstream press reluctant to tell, one of the biggest stories of the war, the massacre of 500 to 600 Vietnamese at the village of My Lai on March 18, 1968.[22] Seymour Hersh, a freelance reporter in Washington, tracked down the story of U.S. soldiers shooting men, women, and children in ditches, but had a hard time getting anyone to publish it. *Life* and *Look* both rejected it before it finally broke into print via syndication by the obscure Dispatch News Service. A full 20 months had elapsed since the atrocities had been committed.[23]

Once the need for real courage was past, major news organizations suddenly recovered theirs and swarmed all over the story. It is the nature of journalism that the deeper the agony, the bigger the headlines. Former correspondent Ward Just touched on the essential parasitism of the press in his novel, *The American Blues* (1984). The narrator admits of himself and other members of the Saigon press corps: "Our enthusiasm for the fall—its blood and dark rhythms, its delusion, the inexorability of the descent, the fulfillment of all the worst prophecies—was almost religious in its intensity."[24]

Earning a living and a professional reputation by recording pain and death, the reporters in Vietnam played a morally ambiguous role that would long haunt many of them. "Perhaps the greatest difference between covering a war and fighting it," Thomas B. Morgan speculated in the July 1984 issue of *Esquire,* "is that, as a correspondent, you don't have to kill anybody. But this only makes the guilt less obvious, not easier to bear."[25] Journalists felt a bruising sense of responsibility for the destruction they witnessed. Peter Arnett of the AP, who spent more time in the field—13 years—than any other correspondent, said:

> ...I think the press corps suffered mass Vietnam stress, and trauma, too, when they came out of there. I think people who'd been in Vietnam a year or more were basically traumatized by what they saw. It affected their thinking and their activities afterwards. Some newsmen committed suicide.... Some lost their careers. I'm sure there's been a greater percentage of failure after Vietnam than after World War II.... It was an unpopular war and the press was affected as the troops were.[26]

Vietnam has a special significance in the gilded history of war correspondence, "for it was there that correspondents began seriously to question the ethics of their business."[27] Rather than hardening them, the cruelties of the war wrung their hearts and seared their consciences. What started out as a job or perhaps a youthful adventure ended as something quite different. In the ironic words of Michael Herr, "I went to cover the war and the war covered me...."[28]

It is no accident, then, that combat reporters and photographers in post-Vietnam films are portrayed as torn between their work and their compassion. Sydney Schanberg, whose reporting experiences formed the basis for *The Killing Fields,* said the war correspondent faces "the ethical paradox of being a human being and a professional observer" at the same time. "You run to the scene," he explained, "and some people are dead and wounded. You scribble notes and snap pictures and at some point you try to decide what you must do. Do you minister to the wounded? Do you give blood? You're required to go back and write a story. Your function is to tell people where you were today, to communicate a scene to them. That is your unspoken oath. But how do you stay human?"[29]

Like the Saigon press corps, the United States emerged from the harrowing complexities of Vietnam less innocent and confident. The war taught Americans that they can't do everything, that their government was capable of lying and murder, that power corrupts. "Vietnamized America was not a proud country," Morgan said in his *Esquire* piece. "In defeat it was ashamed."[30] Yet all that is slowly changing as the war recedes into memory. The black, slab-like Vietnam Veterans Memorial was dedicated in Washington in 1982, and though Southeast Asia still bleeds, officials and editorial writers seized on the occasion as a symbol that America's wounds had finally healed.

A clutch of recent films has assisted in the transformation of the image of the Viet vet from baby killer to forgotten hero.[31] Reflecting the chauvinism of the Reagan years, the films re-fight the Vietnam War and tack a happy ending onto what was undeniably an international calamity. In both *Missing in Action* (1984) and *Rambo: First Blood Part II,* a veteran returns to Vietnam to free U.S. prisoners of war and wreak vengeance on their inhuman captors. If the anti-communist crusade didn't turn out in real life as Americans wished, it can be made to turn out better in the movies. *Rambo,* with its cartoon violence, sadistic villains, and historical amnesia, was one of the top moneymaking films of 1985.

The first major studio movie about the Vietnam War, *The Green Berets,* similarly attempted to cast the conflict in heroic terms. Released in 1968, when there were more than 400,000 U.S. troops in Indochina, the film grossed $8 million at the domestic box office. It did particularly well in the South and Midwest, areas with high recruitment rates. But it also provoked picketing and bombings of the theaters showing it, and was mercilessly pummeled by the critics.[32] "'The Green Berets' is a film so unspeakable, so stupid, so rotten and false in every detail," Renata Adler wrote in the *New York Times*, "that it passes through being fun, through being funny, through being camp, through everything. . . ."[33]

Co-directed by and starring John Wayne, and based on the best seller by Robin Moore, the film is a clumsy monument to racist stereotypes and twisted senile fantasies. Wayne had, in a long screen career, defeated countless red and yellow devils. Now he imposed the demonology and stark moral choices of the Western and the World War II movie on the living agony of Vietnam. Over the entrance to the special forces camp in the film hangs a ranch-style sign that reads "Dodge City." Legions of studio Viet Cong were slaughtered on the set. Michael Wayne, the movie's producer and its star's son, revealingly told an interviewer from *Variety:* "Maybe we shouldn't have destroyed all those Indians, but when you are making a picture the Indians are the bad guys."[34]

Reporters who had seen Vietnam from slit trenches responded sarcastically to the distortions of the film. *The Green Berets* "wasn't really about Vietnam," Michael Herr said, "it was about Santa Monica," a resort city synonymous with sunshine, wealth, and Republicanism.[35] Charles Mohr of the *New York Times* noted that John Wayne was a folk hero, "a kind of reference marker for fictional toughness," to the American boys fighting the war. They called a .45-caliber service pistol a "John Wayne rifle," and the hard, tasteless biscuits in boxes of C rations "John Wayne cookies." Mohr once overheard an exasperated old sergeant tell some troops who were being careless about their lives, "There are two ways to do anything—the right way and the John Wayne way." *The Green Berets,* Mohr said, was filmed "the John Wayne way."[36]

Not the least reason why the movie antagonized correspondents was that it presented them as super unpatriotic. In the opening sequence, a news conference is under way at the John F. Kennedy Center for Special Warfare in North Carolina. Sergeant Muldoon (Aldo Ray) and "Doc" McGee (Raymond St. Jacques) are fielding questions from a group of journalists and ordinary citizens. The reporters don't even bother to hide their liberal biases. "Why is the United States waging this ruthless war?" one asks. The soldiers, who have three tours of duty in Vietnam between them, explain with the sang-froid of Princeton debaters that it is a war against communist domination of the world and display captured Soviet- and Chinese-made weapons to prove it. A housewife then observes: "It's strange that we never read of this in the newspapers." To which Muldoon pointedly replies: "Well, that's newspapers for you, ma'am—you could fill volumes with what you *don't* read in them." This is good for a big laugh from the crowd.

Journalist George Beckworth (David Janssen) winces as Muldoon goes on to compare South Vietnam to the 13 original colonies, and the war to the American Revolution. After the history lesson, Beckworth walks up to Green Beret Colonel Mike Kirby (Wayne), who has been watching the proceedings from the sidelines:

Colonel Mike Kirby (John Wayne) explains the Vietnam War—sort of—to correspondent George Beckworth (David Janssen) in *The Green Berets.*

**Beckworth**: "Your brainwashed sergeant didn't sell me."

**Kirby**: "Didn't sell you what?"

**Beckworth**: "Didn't sell me on the idea that we should be involved in Vietnam."

**Kirby**: "You've ever been to Southeast Asia?"

**Beckworth**: "No, I haven't."

**Kirby**: "Fine."

It is both a put-down and a challenge, and when the colonel and his men arrive at Da Nang airbase, Beckworth shows up right behind them. "I took your suggestion and I came to see for myself," he tells Kirby. He accompanies the Green Berets to an A-team camp (James Lee Barrett's script is infatuated with military jargon and hardware) which is being built in the Viet Cong-infested highlands. And so begins his education in the "realities" of the war.

Beckworth witnesses the torture of a Viet Cong prisoner. It makes him sick and angry. "There is still such a thing as due process," he protests to Kirby. Naturally, he is mistaken. "Out here due process is a bullet," Kirby drawls and, to illustrate, recounts how a Green Beret medic returning from delivering a baby in a Montagnard village was ambushed and beheaded by the VC. Beckworth's face twitches, a sign that he is thinking deeply about what he has just learned.

He has even more to think about after the Viet Cong raid another village, kidnap the young men into their ranks, execute the old chief, and rape and kill the chief's granddaughter. Beckworth had earlier befriended the little girl, giving her a gold chain from around his neck, and her death devastates him. He is now ready to "get with the program," as they used to say in Vietnam.[37]

The Viet Cong launch a night attack on "Dodge City." As mortar rounds explode inside the camp and machine-gun fire crackles, a sergeant yells to Beckworth, "Are you going to stand there and referee, or are you going to help us?" Beckworth doesn't hesitate. He sheds his noncombatant status and passes the ammo.

Despite the bravery of the defenders, the Viet Cong overrun the camp. The Green Berets call in an air strike. Too busy looting the dead to take cover, the VC are cut down, and the camp is recaptured. While the smoke clears, Kirby and Beckworth hold a final talk.

> **Kirby**: "What are you going to say in that newspaper of yours?"
>
> **Beckworth**: "If I say what I feel, I may be out of a job."
>
> **Kirby**: "We'll always give you one."
>
> **Beckworth**: "I can do you more good with a typewriter."

*The Green Berets* labors to portray Vietnam as a holy war, but the film is undone by its internal contradictions. At every opportunity, Kirby fills Beckworth with stories of Viet Cong atrocities. Yet the U.S. soldiers, whatever Wayne intended, scarcely come off as any more admirable. The first order Kirby gives on arriving in camp is to push the jungle back and widen the "killing zone." His men quite enjoy their grisly work—torturing, bombing, shooting, bayoneting, and garroting other human beings. Asked "How come you like blowing things up so much?" Muldoon answers, "When I was a kid, my dad gave me a chemistry set, and it got bigger than both of us." Although meant to be humorous, the explanation sounds psychopathic.

Given the bloodthirstiness and rabid Americanism of the script, it does seem odd that Beckworth's conversion essentially foreshadows the experiences of war correspondents in later, more liberal-minded films. Prompted by his sympathy for the victims of the Viet Cong, Beckworth changes from dove to hawk and vows to battle communism through his reporting. His successors on the screen also are shocked by the death and suffering they see and lose their professional detachment. But it is war itself, not a specific ideology, that is their enemy.

Where *The Green Berets* reduced the Vietnam War to a simple struggle between good and evil, us and them, the post-Vietnam films are full of pain and confusion. The old verities disappeared in the jungles and rice paddies of Southeast Asia. After the My Lai massacre and the secret bombing of Cambodia, it was difficult to believe that goodness and mercy were distinctly American traits. The correspondents in the films of the eighties transfer allegiance from their own kind to the poor and oppressed of all races, nations, and creeds. They are driven by aching consciences to embrace desperate causes and commit dangerous acts.

All the films address complex moral issues, but none with more passion than *The Killing Fields,* which was nominated for an Oscar for best picture of 1984. It is the deeply felt story of the friendship between *New York Times* correspondent Sydney Schanberg and his Cambodian assistant, Dith Pran, played out against a background of civil war and genocide. The film places equal blame for the destruction of Cambodia on the fanaticism of the communist Khmer Rouge and the duplicity of the United States.

For 14 months, beginning in March 1969, American B-52s secretly bombed North Vietnamese and Viet Cong supply dumps in Cambodia (it was no secret, of course, to the villagers the bombs fell on, but it was to the American public). Records of the raids were falsified with the knowledge of President Nixon and high military officers. To escape the attacks, the North Vietnamese and Viet Cong moved their bases deeper into the country, and the war spread. When Nixon went on nationwide TV on April 30, 1970, to announce the ground invasion of Cambodia, he claimed that U.S. policy had been to "scrupulously respect the neutrality of the Cambodian people."[38] *The Killing Fields* damningly intercuts documentary footage of Nixon lying to the public with a heartbreaking, black-and-white procession of soldiers, amputees, corpses, and orphans.

Schanberg, in the January 1980 magazine article that inspired the film, described Cambodia as a "nation pushed into the war by other powers, not in control of its own destiny, being used callously as battle fodder, its agonies largely ignored as the world focused its attention on neighboring Vietnam."[39] After a cease-fire was reached in Vietnam in 1973, the Nixon administration launched all available planes at the Khmer Rouge guerrillas fighting the U.S.-supported government of Lon Nol.[40] The bombing served to increase popular support for the revolution and to further harden the revolutionaries. In April 1975, the Khmer Rouge took over and ruthlessly set about trying to reverse a thousand years of history.

Their leader, Pol Pot, was obsessed with rebuilding the ancient peasant empire of Angkor Wat. The Khmer Rouge declared it the Year Zero. They killed anyone suspected of being an editor, a doctor, a professor. They drove the two million residents of Phnom Penh into the countryside. They bulldozed other cities out of existence. By the time the Vietnamese ousted the Khmer Rouge in 1979, an estimated three million Cambodians, about half the population, had been massacred or had died of starvation or disease.[41] Hence the title, *The Killing Fields.*

The filmmakers went to great lengths to re-create Cambodia's long dark night, and most reviewers agreed with Vincent Canby of the *New York Times* that "the movie looks amazingly authentic."[42] Producer David Puttnam, director Roland Joffe, and screenwriter Bruce Robinson met with Cambodian refugees in the United States, Europe, and Thailand (where the film was mainly shot). The depiction of life in Khmer Rouge communes was drawn from the refugees' recollections and from Yugoslav and East German film footage. Joffe also spoke to State Department experts on Cambodia and read Pol Pot's writings. "One thing I know," said Dith Pran, who endured the terrors of the Khmer Rouge for four years and is now a staff photographer for the *Times*, "this is a true story.... When I see the movie, I say, 'That's past. That's past. Don't give away your tears anymore.' I try to pull myself out, but you cannot pull all the way out. You say, 'Oh my God, I am there again.' "[43]

Dith was played in the film by Dr. Haing S. Ngor, who had never acted before. But Ngor (he puts his surname last in American fashion) lived through the Cambodian bloodletting, and his experiences paralleled those of Dith in the Khmer Rouge work camps. "Only someone who got trapped like me," Dith commented, "could do the part." Ngor's fiancée and virtually all his relatives died under the Khmer Rouge. He himself was jailed three times and tortured, and only survived by denying his past. Like Dith, he eventually escaped into Vietnamese-held territory, and then to Thailand. "I put emotion into the movie," Ngor told an interviewer in his imperfect English. "We have a lot of scenes like in Khmer Rouge time. Everything the same."[44] He won the Oscar for best supporting actor.

Sam Waterston was nominated for the best actor award for his intense performance as Schanberg. In researching the role, Waterston read Schanberg's notebooks and Pulitzer Prize-winning dispatches from Cambodia, and spent time with him and some former *Washington Post* reporters. "I really didn't realize how passionate these people could be about their work," Waterston said. "You know, you get this image of the foreign correspondent as a hard-bitten, international ambulance chaser in a trenchcoat. I knew that wasn't true in Sydney's case but I was shocked to see how wrong it was in general. I don't know why I should have been. I mean, it's only logical that they are professionals who would care deeply and morally about their work."[45]

*The Killing Fields* begins in 1973 and immediately establishes that Schanberg is dedicated and ambitious. When, through a technical blunder, American B-52s drop their big bombs on the little city of Neak Luong, he is determined to tell the world. A U.S. military attache tries to bar him from the area, and Dith warns that it is too dangerous to go. But Schanberg won't be deflected. "This is a big story, a major story," he snaps at his assistant. "We have got to get down there." Stung into action, Dith arranges for them to hitch a ride on a Cambodian patrol boat, and as they travel downriver, Schanberg exults at the prospect of a scoop.

His professional zeal is counterpointed and undercut by the human misery he finds on reaching Neak Luong.

The city is a hell of black smoke, bleeding children, and broken buildings, an example of the insanity that $7 billion worth of bombing can produce. Into the blasted landscape drives a jeep filled with noisy, thuggish Cambodian soldiers and their Khmer Rouge prisoners. The soldiers force their teenage captives to kneel in the rubble and prepare to execute them. Although out of film, Schanberg focuses his camera on the grim tableau in an attempt to forestall the killings. It is a pathetic, if compassionate, gesture. Schanberg and Dith are arrested and hustled away. While the two are still in detention, U.S. officials helicopter the press corps into Neak Luong for a quick, incomplete look at the damage. "They want to sanitize the story," Schanberg screams in outrage.

The movie then flashes forward to 1975 and the collapse of the Lon Nol regime. U.S. officials flee the country, but Schanberg and a handful of other correspondents decide to remain. So does Dith, whose family leaves with the Americans. The stage is set for darkest tragedy.

Without giving any hint of their untapped reserves for violence, the Khmer Rouge enter the capital to the cheers of the populace. "No more fighting, Sydney, no more war," shouts Dith, caught up in the excitement of the moment. Except, the fighting isn't over. It has merely passed into a new phase. The Khmer Rouge suddenly turn their revolution and their weapons against their own people.

In the ensuing holocaust, the journalists are seized and marched off for what seems like certain execution. They watch in horror as the Khmer Rouge coolly torture and kill government soldiers. The atrocities echo the earlier scene at Neak Luong and highlight a central tenet of the film, that bloodshed only begets worse bloodshed. Yet somehow the ingenious Dith persuades the Khmer Rouge to spare the reporters' lives.

The correspondents take refuge at the French embassy. They settle into a kind of dull domestic routine until the Khmer Rouge demand that the Cambodians inside the compound be surrendered to them. There follows a frantic effort to forge a British passport for Dith. It fails, and he must go, probably to his death. "For Christ's sakes,

Sydney, why didn't you get him out when you had the chance?" one of the reporters exclaims. "You had no right to keep him here. You got a funny sense of priorities." Dith defends Schanberg in a voice thick with tears: "I'm a journalist, too, Morgan. I know his heart. I love him like a brother, and I do anything for him, anything."

Dith vanishes into the chaos of Cambodia, and Schanberg returns to New York. At a banquet honoring him as journalist of the year, he runs into photographer Al Rockoff (John Malkovich), another near victim of the Khmer Rouge's blood frenzy. "Know what bothers me?"

Dith Pran (Haing S. Ngor) bids a tearful farewell to photographer Al Rockoff (John Malkovich) and reporter Sydney Schanberg (Sam Waterston, right) in *The Killing Fields.*

Rockoff says. "It bothers me that you let Pran stay in Cambodia because you wanted to win that fucking award." Schanberg, who has been obsessively writing letters to relief groups on the Thai-Cambodian border and otherwise seeking some sign that Dith is still alive, erupts in anger. "This isn't a 1940s movie," he fumes. "You can't just get on a plane and make the whole world come out right." However that may be, he later admits to his sister and himself: "I never really gave [Dith] any choice. One time he tried to discuss leaving. I talked to him about it. But we never really discussed it. He stayed because I wanted him to stay. I stayed because. . . ." The confession trails off into silence, as if the truth were too terrible to share with any but the damned.

Finally, in 1979, after surviving a nightmare of loneliness, hunger, and cruelty, Dith emerges from behind the black curtain the Khmer Rouge have drawn around Cambodia. The friends are reunited amid the squalor of a refugee camp. As they sway in each other's embrace, the John Lennon song, "Imagine," soars on the soundtrack ("Imagine there's no country/ It isn't hard to do/ Nothing to kill or die for. . . ."). "Forgive me?" Schanberg asks. "Nothing to forgive, nothing," Dith says. In a twinkling, we have been magically transported from the bomb craters and mass graves of Cambodia to the sweet land of Hollywood romance.

Regardless of its syrupy ending, *The Killing Fields* is a profoundly political film, if politics means, as one scholar suggested, "our chances to live together and not to lie."[46] It is also a gruesome film to watch. We see people shredded by bullets and bombs, and suffocated with plastic bags. The horrific images of violence and pain are inseparable from the film's humanitarian message. In a particularly haunting scene, Schanberg and other correspondents visit a hospital jammed with civilian casualties of the fighting. There is blood on the floor, on the walls—everywhere but where it belongs. A British doctor, tending to a little girl with shrapnel in her spine, asks from the depths of his weariness and despair, "How many corpses have to be piled up before people say it's time to go home?" The question embarrasses the reporters, and they shuffle out of the hospital with heavy consciences.

Schanberg comes through the butchery morally regenerated. The ordeal of Cambodia awakens his sense of responsibility for the castoffs of war. He says in his acceptance speech at the awards banquet that the men who ordered the secret bombing were concerned about many things, but that they were "specifically not concerned with the Cambodian people... except in the abstract, as instruments of policy." Whether it is America's exploitation of Cambodia or his own of Dith, evil flows from treating others merely as means and not as ends. *The Killing Fields* is, ultimately, a plea for unconditional, godlike love, love that doesn't discriminate between yellow and white, educated and peasant, communist and anti-communist.

And it is a plea to remember. After the Khmer Rouge took control of Cambodia, they diagnosed memory as a sickness and sought to purge it with fire and blood. The film summons the ghosts out of the shadows, tells what they saw and suffered that they might not have suffered in vain.

*The Year of Living Dangerously,* unlike *The Killing Fields* or *The Green Berets,* isn't directly about the U.S. involvement in Southeast Asia. It opens with Australian reporter Guy Hamilton (Mel Gibson) arriving in Jakarta in 1965 to cover the tottering Sukarno regime. Every day brings new rumors of an impending coup. To placate the communists, President Sukarno offers to sanction a communist army. Right-wing Moslem generals, with the connivance of the West, resist. Peking sends a shipload of arms to its Indonesian supporters. Bureaucratic corruption is rampant, and in the streets, people are starving.

Hamilton looks on the turmoil as an opportunity to make a name for himself. "Ten years I've waited for this," he says, "and if I mess it up, it's back to the newsroom in Sydney, and that's a bloody graveyard." He gets off to a shaky start. His first broadcast is greeted by the home office with the acid comment, "Guy, that wasn't news, it was travelogue."

He receives unexpected help from Eurasian cameraman Billy Kwan (Linda Hunt in an Oscar-winning performance), who leads him by the hand to exclusive stories. The mysterious Kwan keeps dossiers on all the people he knows. In his file on Hamilton, he writes: "I felt sorry for you, dumped into your first overseas posting without contacts, adrift, trying to bluff your way through." Moreover, he senses in Hamilton a potential soulmate. "Could you be the unmet friend?" he wonders. The parallel to Schanberg and Dith is obvious—and intriguing.

At the mythic core of both *The Year of Living Dangerously* and *The Killing Fields* is an asexual romance between male buddies. So-called "buddy pictures" enjoyed a considerable vogue after the success of *Butch Cassidy and the Sundance Kid* (1969), starring Paul Newman and Robert Redford.[47] But the "marriages" between Hamilton and Kwan, and between Schanberg and Dith, are more than an attempt to recapture yesterday's box-office magic. They follow the archetypical pattern outlined by Leslie Fiedler in his 1948 essay, "Come Back to the Raft Ag'in, Huck Honey!"

Fiedler, then the *enfant terrible* of literary criticism, argued that the mutual love of a white man and a colored is a central theme of classic American literature. He cited Natty Bumppo and Chingachgook in Cooper; Ishmael and Queequeg in Melville; Huck and Nigger Jim in Twain.[48] The post-Vietnam films embody the same myths, rooted in a yearning for the transhistorical reconciliation of racial and cultural opposites. Moved by an inexplicable tenderness, a native befriends a Western correspondent and absolves him of the sins of his race, centuries of subjugation and slaughter. But the dynamics of the past insidiously extend into the present and aren't to be mitigated or evaded. In Kwan, who is half-Chinese, half-Australian, East and West meet—or, more exactly, collide: he is deformed, a dwarf. The films dramatize the colored man as the trusting victim of his white brother. Because of Schanberg, Dith is plunged into the darkness that was Cambodia, and because of Hamilton, Kwan dies a martyr. The dream of reconciliation is just that, a dream, and dreams fade.

Directed by Australian Peter Weir and based on an Australian novel by C.J. Koch, *The Year of Living Dan-*

*gerously* is, among other things, a portrait of a strange, extravagantly complex culture that tempts, bewilders, and finally defeats Westerners. "It's confusing to visit Southeast Asia," Weir said, "it's overwhelming. Every sense is being hit with information; you're battered with sights and sounds and smells, and you can't quite add it all up. You think you've got hold of something, and you lose it."[49] Or, as Kwan aphorizes, "Most of us become children again when we enter the slums of Asia."

Critics had described the mood of Weir's earlier films—*The Last Wave, Gallipoli,* and *Picnic at Hanging Rock*—as "disquieting," "elusive," and "ominous," terms that also apply to *The Year of Living Dangerously.*[50] Bernard Kalb, who covered Indonesia for the *New York Times* in the late fifties and early sixties, said the movie was "a couple of hours of living impatiently with a caricature of a coup attempt laid to the Communists. . . ." Yet even he conceded that "at moments during the film, I felt I was back there again, amid the anti-West slogans; the massive anti-American demonstrations in front of the U.S. embassy; the all-night *wayang* shadow plays; the tinkling music of the *gamelon;* the *real,* giant Sukarno posters dominating the landscape. . . ."[51]

The title is never explained in the film. It was actually Sukarno's own phrase. The Indonesian strongman used to give each year a name in order to channel the energy and will of his people toward a common goal. In 1957 it was "The Year of Decision"; in 1958 "The Year of Challenge"; in 1959 "The Year of the Rediscovery of the Revolution."[52] "He said 1965 would be the year of living dangerously," Weir recalled in an interview, "as Indonesia tried to become independent [of the West] and go it alone, and prophetically that turned out to be true for Sukarno himself."[53]

Absorbed in covering palace politics, advancing their careers, and pursuing their private pleasures, the correspondents in the film shrug off the misery in the streets. Kwan "adopts" Hamilton in hopes of transforming him into a "virtuous journalist," one whose work is founded on a concern for the dispossessed.[54] Throughout the film, Kwan points to the desperate poverty of millions of Indonesians and asks, "What then must we do?" His own answer is, "We must give with love to anyone God places in our path." But to the reporters, that is naive. "We can't afford to get involved," they say. Kwan would say we can't afford not to, if we want to stay human.

Although Hamilton is more intelligent and caring than the other Western journalists (one sleeps with dollar prostitutes, another with boys), his moral education is pretty much a failure. This becomes apparent in his romance with Jill Bryant (Sigourney Weaver), an assistant to the military attache at the British embassy. Kwan loves Jill, but can't have her, and so presents her to Hamilton. Their passion smolders for a while, then blazes up in a scene in which they run out of an embassy dinner party, leap into his car, and smash through an army roadblock in their hurry to get to a hotel room. As Vincent Canby observed, "That, my friends, is heat."[55]

But Hamilton never stops playing reporter, not even in bed. One night after love-making, Jill discloses to him the contents of a top-secret message the embassy has received.

> **Bryant:** "A ship left Shanghai a few days ago with arms for the PKI" [the Indonesian Communist Party].
>
> **Hamilton:** "Civil war."
>
> **Bryant:** "Yes. . . . Look, I'm not telling you this to give you some fantastic scoop. I just want you to save your life. If the PKI take over, they'll slaughter every European in Jakarta. . . . "
>
> **Hamilton:** "Jill, I'm staying. . . . Nothing will keep the Communists and Moslems apart now. . . . When are they going to get the stuff?"
>
> **Bryant:** "God, you can't use this."
>
> **Hamilton:** "Then you shouldn't have told me."

So blinded is Hamilton by ambition that he can't see that he is doing anything unethical. Kwan tries to persuade him to drop the story, insisting that Jill gave it to him off the record. Hamilton counters that he won't broadcast it unless he can get independent confirmation. "Great," Kwan gibes, "that should ease your conscience," and adds that if the PKI finds out what he is seeking, he is a dead man. But Kwan's warnings are lost on the scoop-crazed reporter. "If I don't follow something like this up," Hamilton says, "I might as well go and grow watermelons."

Kwan had thought that Hamilton was potentially "a man of light," but no more. "You have changed," he writes in his former protégé's file. "You are capable of betrayal. You abuse your position as journalist and grow addicted to risk. You attempt to draw neat lines around yourself, making a fetish of your career and making all relationships temporary lest they disturb that career."

Of all the characters in the film, only Kwan, the sad little freak, is capable of selflessness, the grand gesture. To publicize the starvation and suffering, as the press won't, he unfurls a banner saying "Sukarno Feed Your People" from the window of a hotel at which the president is scheduled to deliver a speech. Security men burst into the room, throw Kwan out the window, and haul in the banner. Hamilton, waiting in a mob of reporters on the sidewalk for Sukarno's arrival, sees Kwan fall and rushes to him. A faint smile flickers across Kwan's face as Hamilton cradles his head, and then he dies. The correspondent's hands are red with blood.

More blood flows before the film is over, including Hamilton's own. The long-predicted communist revolt erupts. Hamilton, fearing for his life, leaves for the airport. Nervous soldiers stop his car at a barricade outside the presidential palace. When he protests, he is struck with a rifle butt and seriously injured. His driver takes him to Kwan's bungalow and abandons him. With both eyes bandaged, he lies helplessly in bed, imagining voices and expecting to be murdered at any moment.

Another of Hamilton's assistants, a member of the PKI, suddenly appears—not to kill him, but to tell him that the coup has been crushed by the Moslem generals. Hamilton rips off his bandages and demands to be driven

Correspondent Guy Hamilton (Mel Gibson) and his Indonesian assistant (Bembol Roco) in *The Year of Living Dangerously.*

to the airport. "Why do you have to leave now?" the assistant asks. "You can stay and write all the stories you want...." But Hamilton has had his fill of the world of foreign correspondence, where reporters gamble with their nerves and brains to win front-page bylines and bigger assignments. The glamor and excitement of it all are overrated. On his way to the airport, he sees soldiers machine-gunning communists and communist suspects along the roadside. It is the beginning of a bloodbath that eventually would claim hundreds of thousands of lives. The film ends with Hamilton walking onto a plane and into Jill's arms. He has clawed his way out from under the rubble of his ambition.

Bernard Kalb found the whole thing preposterous. He said he just couldn't believe that a correspondent who had waited ten years—"count'em"—for an overseas assignment would turn his back on a major story.[56] But Kalb, like most journalists commenting on journalism films, was too literal in his interpretation. *The Year of Living Dangerously* is a volatile political allegory. In criticizing the film for not sticking to the facts, Kalb ignored its symbolic truths. He brought to his evaluation of the characters and their motives the scoop mentality the film repudiates as empty and inhuman.

While kinder in his review, Vincent Canby wasn't totally accurate either when he called *The Year of Living Dangerously* "a good, romantic melodrama."[57] It may be that, but it is also something more. It is a film about impassable cultural barriers, about disillusionment and death, about people who, in Kwan's words, "will become other people, who will become old, betray their dreams, become ghosts."

No matter in which country or year they are set, the recent films that probe the morality of war correspondence all seem to ultimately refer to the U.S. experience in Southeast Asia. *Under Fire,* which focuses on three crack American journalists caught up in the Nicaraguan revolution of 1979, vividly reflects the legacy of shame and guilt growing out of the Vietnam War. Like *The Year of Living Dangerously* and *The Killing Fields,* the movie shows correspondents struggling to cope both professionally and personally with large-scale suffering. By having two of the protagonists side with the victims of the repressive Somoza regime, it provides vicarious restitution for the mistakes of Vietnam and the historic blood lust of the press.

Filmed in Mexico on an $8 million budget, *Under Fire* was directed by Roger Spottiswoode and written by Clayton Frohman and Ron Shelton. Spottiswoode and Shelton traveled to Nicaragua, where they interviewed correspondents and added a number of anecdotes to the script, including one about a young Sandinista who idolizes the Baltimore Orioles and can throw grenades with the accuracy of a major league pitcher.[58]

The film created controversy even before going into commercial release. In August 1983 the National Press Club in Washington invited its 3,000 members to a screening of the picture. Then word spread that the film glorified the Sandinista revolution (which the Reagan administration was striving mightily to reverse), and that it suggested that some reporters who covered the fighting supported the rebels. Facing embarrassment, the club hastened to announce in its September 15 bulletin: "The National Press Club is not sponsoring the movie 'Under Fire' or any other movie, nor was permission asked to use the National Press Club name on the invitations that members received."

A club member had approved the invitations, but the disavowal got wide circulation, anyway. The conservative National Center for Public Policy incorporated it into a flier that was distributed outside the theater the night of the preview. The flier accused the makers of *Under Fire* of "subterfuge by appropriating the National Press Club's name to promote their film," and of giving favorable treatment to "a revolution based on tyrannical dictatorship."[59]

The specter of slanted news coverage of the Nicaraguan civil war had first been raised more than a year earlier by Shirley Christian in the pages of the *Washington Journalism Review.* Christian, a Latin American correspondent for the *Miami Herald* and winner of the 1981 Pulitzer Prize for international reporting, analyzed hundreds of stories produced by the *Washington Post,* the *New York Times,* and CBS News during the revolution. She found that the press, in its hatred of Anastasio Somoza and his brutal National Guard, had misrepresented or ignored the Marxist ideology of the Sandinista leaders. "The American media, like most of the United States, went on a guilt trip in Nicaragua," she said. Reporters were trying to live down the memory of Vietnam, trying to atone for the previous blunders of U.S. foreign policy. "Obsessed with the past," she wrote, "journalists were unable, or unwilling, to see the tell-tale signs of the future."[60]

What distinguishes *Under Fire* from other war correspondent films isn't that it explores the dilemma inherent in being a professional observer while all around you people are suffering and dying, but that it proposes a radical solution to the problem. It plainly implies that there comes a time when a correspondent must shed his objectivity and act. The film, at least in this regard, recalls

Graham Greene's novel, *The Quiet American* (1955), in which Fowler, a jaded British reporter in Vietnam, learns that "[w]e all take sides in a moment of emotion and then we cannot get out."[61]

At the beginning of *Under Fire,* the main characters are entirely indifferent to the rights and wrongs of the conflicts they cover. Freelance photographer Russel Price (Nick Nolte), *Time* magazine correspondent Alex Grozier (Gene Hackman), and radio reporter Claire Stryder (Joanna Cassidy) are action junkies on a manic search for a bigger high, a more potent fix of violence. The film draws a parallel between them and Oates (Ed Harris), an American mercenary who drifts from war to war, fighting for whichever side pays the best. After a stint in strife-torn Chad, they all race off to the latest flash point, Nicaragua. "I hear it's a neat little war and a nice hotel," Alex says.

But something happens to Claire and Russel under

Combat photographer Russel Price (Nick Nolte) sprints for cover in *Under Fire.*

the pressure of events in Nicaragua—they fall in love with each other and the revolution. Their newly aroused political sympathies soon collide head-on with their journalistic duties. They are lured to a Sandinista hideout with the promise that they will be allowed to take the first-ever photographs of the guerrilla leader Rafael, only to discover Rafael is dead. The rebels want Russel to photograph him in such a way that the Carter administration will believe that he is still alive, and so cancel further aid to Somoza. "I'm a journalist," Russel says, meaning he doesn't do things like that. "This has nothing to do with journalism," a Sandinista replies. "Enough of our people have been lost already."

While Russel wrestles with his conscience, Claire says of the picture he may or may not take, "Sure would be a prize winner, wouldn't it?"

> **Russel:** "I've won enough prizes."
>
> **Claire:** "But you've never won a war."

He takes the picture.

"I think I finally saw one too many bodies," Russel later offers in explanation. The film asks a lot—in fact, too much for Vincent Canby—when it asks us to accept that case-hardened journalists could lose their detachment so suddenly and completely. Canby termed *Under Fire* "the perfect film for everyone who distrusts the press."[62]

The filmmakers leave little doubt that they, at any rate, consider the fabrication ethically justified by the extraordinary circumstances in which Russel finds himself. The background music swells as copies of the fake photograph circulate throughout the country and the masses rally to the revolutionary cause. Yet Russel's romance with the Sandinistas also has unintended and bloody consequences, which the film doesn't shrink from presenting. Other pictures Russel took at the hideout fall into hands of the National Guard, helping them to round up and execute many rebels. And Alex, who had gone to New York to become a TV anchorman, now returns to Nicaragua in quest of an interview with Rafael. In an echo of the actual killing of ABC correspondent Bill Stewart, he is shot to death by Somoza's uniformed thugs.

Alex's murder leads to the following exchange between a tearful Claire and a Nicaraguan doctor at an overcrowded Red Cross field hospital. Nothing in the other post-Vietnam films quite equals the woman doctor's cold, concentrated contempt for foreign correspondents. Her words reveal the pent-up bitterness and frustration of a people whose sufferings have been overlooked or misreported, whose dreams of justice still wait to be told:

> **Doctor:** "Fifty thousand Nicaraguans have died and now one Yankee. Perhaps now Americans will be outraged at what is happening here."
>
> **Claire:** "Perhaps they will."
>
> **Doctor:** "Maybe we should have killed an American journalist fifty years ago."

After two hours of showing bombings, bodies, and betrayals, the film ends on an upbeat note. Somoza flees to Miami and the "revolution of poets" triumphs. Watching the Sandinistas enter the capital to the cheers of the populace, Claire asks Russel, "Do you think we fell in love with too much?" He answers, "I'd do it again."

*Under Fire,* despite failing to provide its protagonists with credible inner lives, does succeed in conveying the wild, superheated atmosphere in which foreign correspondents operate—the competition, the camaraderie, the big talk, the small talk. It takes deliberate aim at the pseudocolor and clichés that often substitute for insight in overseas reporting. Among the minor characters is a TV correspondent who, unfortunately, might have stepped right out of the evening news. Clad in the mandatory bush jacket for a "stand-up" on the roof of a Managua hotel, he holds his microphone at a professional angle, looks meaningfully into the camera, and delivers inanities like "This tiny nation of smoldering volcanoes erupted in fighting today. . . ."

The central theme of *Under Fire,* as somewhat less overtly of *The Killing Fields* and *The Year of Living Dangerously,* is that there can be no neutrals in the struggle between freedom and tyranny. All the films mock the notion of war as a test of manhood and overturn the image of the war correspondent as a red-blooded hero. Alex is cast from the old heroic mold. He insults his editor, dodges grenades, and chases after scoops. His death implies that traditional journalistic values have become irrelevant. There are too many innocent victims for war to be treated as a "helluva story."

Interestingly, but perhaps not surprisingly, post-Vietnam novels about war correspondence follow much the same pattern as the films. In *DelCorso's Gallery* (1983) by Philip Caputo, Nick DelCorso argues that it is "his job, and every combat photographer's job, to put themselves out of business." He feels compelled to alert people through his pictures to the monstrousness of war. "To seize them by the throat and scream, This is what we are doing to each other."[63] At the root of his compulsion is the guilty memory of a massacre he photographed in Vietnam a decade ago, firing his camera as cruelly and indiscriminately as the U.S. soldiers had fired their rifles.

The unnamed narrator of Ward Just's *The American Blues* also is entangled in the tortured shadows of the past. He had been a member of the Saigon press corps, one of the "[c]onnoisseurs of bad news," a role that still gnaws at his conscience. "There was no equity," he now admits, "in an agony where only the observers profited."[64] As penance, he is writing a history of the war, or trying to:

> I told my wife, I can't end this book.
> You have got to let it go, she said.
> The book? I asked incredulously. She couldn't know what she was asking.
> The war, she said furiously.[65]

If there is a key difference between the novels and films, it is in their dénouements. DelCorso is killed while photographing the Lebanese civil war. Just's narrator returns to Vietnam, seeking his last chapter, his summing-up. But the trip is a failure. He doesn't find any answers, only more questions, and is left grappling inconclusively with his demons. By comparison, the films have old-fashioned happy endings. Friends/lovers are reunited in the closing minutes of *The Killing Fields* and *The Year of Living Dangerously,* and a ruthless tyrant comes crashing down in *Under Fire.* The films don't risk the bleak or ambiguous endings that their grim stories would seem to dictate.

In F. Scott Fitzgerald's Hollywood novel, *The Last Tycoon* (1941), movie producer Monroe Stahr says, "Our condition is that we have to take people's own favorite folklore and dress it up and give it back to them."[66] The war correspondent films of the 1980s embody the guilt and doubt of "Vietnamized America." And yet, for all their blood-soaked images of man's inhumanity to man, they contrive to leave audiences with the impression that everything is going to work out fine. It is as if the filmmakers were suggesting that our crisis of the spirit is finally over; that, having sat for a couple of hours in a dark movie theater and felt sympathy for the small, impoverished countries ground between the contending wills of the two superpowers, we are released from further self-recrimination. Hooray for Hollywood, indeed!

But exploring even in a safely proscribed way our responsibility as a nation for the endless series of riots, revolutions, and proxy wars around the globe is, at best, an awkward business. Most people don't want to hear about it, and movies that bring it up may be going out of style, if they were ever actually in style. The latest war correspondent film, *Salvador,* barely made it into release, got mixed reviews, and sank quickly from sight.[67]

Based on the experiences of freelance journalist Richard Boyle, who did the script with director Oliver Stone, the film graphically portrays the torture cells, right-wing death squads, and body dumps of the civil war in El Salvador. At first, the lawlessness of the place holds a certain perverse appeal for Boyle (James Woods), a burned-out veteran of the coverage of Vietnam and other hot spots. "You're gonna love it here, Doc," he assures a new arrival. "You can drive drunk and get anybody killed for 50 bucks." Later, as colleagues and acquaintances fall victim to the reign of terror, he loses his cynical detachment. He finds himself moved by the plight of the Salvadorans and shamed by the extent of Washington's complicity in their repression and murder. He tells U.S. embassy officials, "All you're doing is bringing misery to these people."

Sydney Schanberg, Guy Hamilton, and Russel Price are modern professionals. Boyle more properly belongs to a bygone era of journalism—and journalism films—when newspaper work was considered a refuge for failures and misfits. Brash and boozy and perpetually broke, he is a direct descendant of the scrofulous newspapermen in *The Front Page* (1931). That one such as he would develop a sense of shame represents something of a climax in the evolution of the sub-genre. The newshawks in the films of the thirties and forties were blind to the drift of history and deaf to cries for mercy, and proud of it. *Salvador* generates narrative tension by investing the archetypical hard-drinking, fast-talking reporter with the rudiments of a soul. But the film's vaguely left-wing politics and dire insistence that the U.S. involvement in El Salvador threatens a tragic rerun of Vietnam proved poison at the box office.

*Salvador* received belated recognition after *Platoon,* also written and directed by Stone, was released in mid-December 1986 and became a critical and commercial success.[68] The enthusiasm for *Platoon,* which *Time* called "the most impressive movie to deal with the fighting in Viet Nam," spilled over onto *Salvador.*[69] Boyle and Stone were nominated for an Oscar for best screenplay, and Woods for best actor. Although *Salvador* was shut out at the Academy Awards, *Platoon* was voted best picture, and Stone, a Vietnam veteran, best director.

It is possible that *Platoon* signals a new willingness on the part of Hollywood and the public to see the Vietnam War whole and in daylight, but unlikely. For one thing, the film itself romanticizes the men who fought and died in the war. "They're the best there is... ," the narrator, a college dropout who volunteered for the infantry, claims, "the heart and soul." For another, its grunt's-eye view of the war is politically and morally limited, if not precisely excusing the massacres and rapes committed by the soldiers, then at least attributing the atrocities to understandable grief and rage at the sneak killings of their comrades. *Platoon* isn't so much about the agony Americans inflicted on Vietnam as about the agony Vietnam inflicted on Americans. The suffering of the Vietnamese people is almost incidental to the tragedy. The film seems peculiarly blind to who was the aggressor in Southeast Asia. Consciously seeking to allay 20 years of guilt, it asks us to honor the heroism, dignity, and endurance of foot soldiers trapped in a war they never wanted.[70]

Vincent Canby, in a "think piece" in the Sunday *New York Times,* observed that *Platoon* "comes out of a long tradition of 'war' movies—everything from 'Battleground' to (don't laugh) 'The Green Berets.'" He added that "in spite of its sense of desolation, [the film] could well inspire the fantasies of some future generations of American soldiers." He saw it one afternoon at Loew's Astor Plaza, where "there was a small but noisy claque that kept trying to respond to the film's reluctant heroes, and to its grim battle footage, as if 'Platoon' were another 'Rambo.'"[71] Soon they had Rambo himself to cheer again. *Rambo III*, in which America's favorite avenger invades Soviet-held Afghanistan, was released in the summer of 1988. Sylvester Stallone, its star and director, announced during filming, "Rambo will always remain the way he was created, unpredictable and explosive, but totally patriotic."[72]

Everywhere there are signs of the so-called "Rambo mentality." When U.S. planes bombed Libya in April 1986 in retaliation for the Arab country's support of international terrorism, American allies in Europe denounced the raid as counterproductive, but Americans themselves overwhelmingly endorsed it. And why not? It was like another of the slam-bang, militaristic movie fantasies—*Top Gun* or *Delta Force* (both 1986)—so popular with contemporary audiences.[73]

"The essential American soul," D.H. Lawrence once wrote, "is hard, isolate, stoic, and a killer."[74] We are addicted to dark, bloody dreams. The causes of the addiction are buried deep in our history and our psyches, in our frontier heritage and our impatience with social forms. We identify most closely with film heroes capable of sudden and terrible violence. The world is a savage place, and we thrill with excitement and relief when a Wayne or an Eastwood or a Stallone smites our enemies with a mighty arm, and then coolly strides away from the slaughter.

War correspondents in films of the eighties plead for decency and compassion toward other peoples. But our ideal selves, as reflected on the screen, are men who spread destruction, not understanding. We long to escape our fears through the explosive release of immediate, unequivocal action. Full of anxiety and suspicion, we approach the rest of the world with a gun in our hands. A line from *The Green Berets* comes back like the echo of a gunshot: "Out here due process is a bullet." Our hard-faced heroes teach that death will cleanse the earth faster and more thoroughly than love.

## Notes

1. Rudyard Kipling, *The Light That Failed* (Garden City, N.Y.: Doubleday, 1899), p. 20. For a fuller discussion of the literary image of war correspondents, see the author's "The Image of War Correspondents in Anglo-American Fiction," *Journalism Monographs,* no. 97, June 1986.
2. Stephen Crane, *Active Service* (New York: International Association of Newspapers and Authors, 1901), p. 120.
3. Alex Barris, *Stop the Presses!: The Newspaperman in American Films* (South Brunswick, N.J.: A.S. Barnes, 1976), p. 103.
4. Michael Arlen, *Living-Room War* (New York: Viking Press, 1969), p. 106.
5. Ward Just, *The American Blues* (New York: Viking Press, 1984), p. 196.

6. Michael Herr, *Dispatches* (New York: Avon Books, 1978), pp. 234–35.

7. Frederick Palmer, *With My Own Eyes* (Indianapolis: Bobbs-Merrill, 1933), pp. 41–42.

8. Rupert Furneaux, *The First War Correspondent: William Howard Russell of the Times* (London: Cassell, 1945), pp. 219–20.

9. John Keegan, *The Face of War* (New York: Viking Press, 1976), p. 240.

10. William L. Shirer, *20th Century Journey: The Nightmare Years, 1930–1940,* vol. 2 (Boston: Little, Brown, 1984), p. 508.

11. Francis McCullagh, "The Question of the War Correspondent," *Contemporary Review,* CIII, February 1913, p. 209.

12. Herbert L. Matthews, *The Education of a Correspondent* (New York: Harcourt, Brace, 1946), p. 9.

13. William L. O'Neill, *Coming Apart: An Informal History of America in the 1960's* (New York: Quadrangle Books, 1971), p. 333.

14. *Ibid.*

15. Quoted in Edwin Emery and Michael Emery, *The Press and America: An Interpretive History of the Mass Media,* 5th ed. (Englewood Cliffs, N.J.: Prentice-Hall, 1984), p. 613.

16. *Ibid.*, p. 563.

17. M.L. Stein, *Under Fire: The Story of American War Correspondents* (New York: Messner, 1968), p. 84.

18. Herr, *Dispatches,* p. 244.

19. Emery and Emery, *Press and America,* p. 564; James Boylan, "Declarations of Independence," *Columbia Journalism Review,* 25th Anniversary Issue, November/December 1986, p. 35.

20. O'Neill, *Coming Apart,* p. 330.

21. Emery and Emery, *Press and America,* pp. 561–63.

22. *Time* magazine commissioned pollster Louis Harris to find out what Americans thought of the incident. Most were sympathetic to the soldiers who were brought up on charges by the Army and blamed the media for reporting the massacre. O'Neill, *Coming Apart,* p. 402.

23. Emery and Emery, *Press and America,* p. 609; Boylan, "Declarations of Independence," p. 36.

24. Just, *American Blues,* p. 30.

25. Thomas B. Morgan, "Reporters of the Lost War," *Esquire,* July 1984, p. 60.

26. Quoted in *ibid.,* p. 54.

27. Phillip Knightley, *The First Casualty* (New York: Harcourt Brace Jovanovich, 1975), p. 408.

28. Herr, *Dispatches,* p. 20.

29. Quoted in Jane Gross, "Movies and the Press Are an Enduring Romance," *New York Times,* 2 June 1985, sec. 2, p. 19.

30. Morgan, "Reporters of Lost War," p. 55.

31. Whether the critically acclaimed *Platoon* (1986) signals the start of a counter trend toward greater realism in films about Vietnam is discussed later in this chapter.

32. Gilbert Adair, *Vietnam on Film* (n.p.: Proteus, 1981), pp. 15, 52.

33. Renata Adler, *New York Times Film Reviews* (New York: New York Times and Arno Books, 1970), 1959–1968, p. 3765.

34. Quoted in Adair, *Vietnam on Film,* p. 25.

35. Herr, *Dispatches,* p. 200.

36. Charles Mohr, *New York Times Film Reviews* (New York: New York Times and Arno Books, 1970), 1959–1968, p. 3766.

37. *Ibid.*

38. Emery and Emery, *Press and America,* p. 610.

39. Sydney Schanberg, *The Death and Life of Dith Pran* (New York: Penguin Books, 1985), p. 3. Originally published in *New York Times Magazine,* 20 January 1980.

40. Anthony Lewis, "We Must Remember," *New York Times,* 13 December 1984, sec. 1, p. 31.

41. *Ibid.;* Samuel G. Freedman, "In 'The Killing Fields,' a Cambodian Actor Relives His Nation's Ordeal," *New York Times,* 28 October 1984, sec. 2, p. 1.

42. Vincent Canby, "Tale of Death and Life of a Cambodian," *New York Times,* 2 November 1984, sec. 3, p. 23.

43. Freedman, "Actor Relives Nation's Ordeal," pp. 1, 17.

44. *Ibid.*

45. Quoted in Desmond Ryan, "The Hollywood Reporter," *Washington Journalism Review,* September 1985, p. 47.

46. Frank D. McConnell, *The Spoken Seen* (Baltimore: Johns Hopkins University Press, 1975), p. 111.

47. Les Keyser, *Hollywood in the Seventies* (San Diego: A.S. Barnes, 1981), p. 38.

48. Leslie Fiedler, *A Fiedler Reader* (New York: Stein and Day, 1977), pp. 5–7, 12.

49. Quoted in Leslie Bennetts, "East and West Meet Amid Mystery in Peter Weir's New Film," *New York Times,* 16 January 1983, sec. 2, p. 23.

50. *Ibid.*

51. Bernard Kalb, "Cinematic Art vs. Reality in Indonesia," *New York Times,* 23 January 1983, sec. 2, p. 17.

52. *Ibid.*

53. Quoted in Bennetts, "East and West Meet," p. 23.

54. See Michael J. Kirkhorn, "The Virtuous Journalist: An Exploratory Essay," *Quill,* February 1982, pp. 9–23.

55. Vincent Canby, "Year of Living Dangerously," *New York Times,* 21 January 1983, p. C4.

56. Kalb, "Cinematic Art vs. Reality," p. 22.

57. Canby, "Year of Living Dangerously," p. C4.

58. Richard Bernstein, "Issues Raised by 'Under Fire,'" *New York Times,* 30 October 1983, sec. 2, pp. 9–10.

59. *New York Times,* 3 October 1983, p. B10.

60. Shirley Christian, "Covering the Sandinistas," *Washington Journalism Review,* March 1982, p. 38.

61. Graham Greene, *The Quiet American* (London: William Heinemann, 1955; reprint ed., New York: Penguin Books, 1981), p. 152.

62. Vincent Canby, "Reporters Are A Continuing Story for Moviemakers," *New York Times,* 18 November 1984, sec. 2, p. 20.

63. Philip Caputo, *DelCorso's Gallery* (New York: Holt, Rinehart and Winston, 1983), p. 62.

64. Just, *American Blues,* p. 7.

65. *Ibid.,* pp. 14–15.

66. F. Scott Fitzgerald, *The Last Tycoon* (New York: Charles Scribner's Sons, 1941), p. 105.

67. Marshall Fine of the Gannett News Service called *Salvador* "one of the year's most overlooked films." But after flopping in general theatrical release, the film has found a second life in art houses and on videocassette. Fine, "The Best and Worst Films of '86: One critic's choice," *Poughkeepsie Journal,* 2 January 1987, p. 4D.

68. *Platoon* had earned more than $100 million three months after its release. This, of course, didn't go unnoticed in Hollywood, which released four more Vietnam War films in 1987–88. Meanwhile, CBS unveiled the first Vietnam-related weekly TV series, "Tour of Duty," in the fall of 1987. John J. O'Connor, TV critic for the *New York Times,* called it the "most astonishing denial of reality" to be found among the programs of the new television season. "Ignoring such sensitive subjects as the extensive war protests at home and the problems of drugs among the soldiers at the front," he wrote, "this show wants to offer tidy inspirational essays on kinship and brotherhood.... The result is history in the World War II mold, complete with a Rambo-like sergeant who each week performs enough heroics to merit any normal 'grunt' several Medals of Honor." "Television Tests Its Limits," *New York Times,* 11 October 1987, sec. 2, p. 35; Harry F. Waters, "Prime Time for Vietnam," *Newsweek,* August 31, 1987. pp. 68–69.

69. Richard Corliss, "A Document Written in Blood," *Time,* December 15, 1986, p. 83.

70. It seems to me—admittedly, I may be premature in my judgment; certainly, I am almost alone in it—that *Platoon* belongs to the mainstream of recent efforts, in and out of the movies, to "indemnify" Vietnam veterans and, by extension, bowdlerize the history of the war. The film would never have had the success it had if it didn't reinforce the prevailing values and attitudes of the Reagan years. In a speech at Arlington National Cemetery on Memorial Day 1986, President Reagan referred to the U.S. soldiers in Vietnam as "quite a group... boys who fought a terrible and vicious war without enough support from home, boys who were dodging bullets while we debated the efficacy of battle." The front-page headline in *USA Today* ("The Nation's Newspaper") over the story reporting Reagan's speech read, "Forgotten Viet heroes recognized." *USA Today,* 27 May 1986, p. 1A.

71. Vincent Canby, "'Platoon' Finds New Life in Old War Movies," *New York Times,* 11 January 1987, sec. 2, p. 21.

72. For a discussion of the cultural significance of Stallone's popularity and film persona, see Steven D. Stark, "10 Years Into the Stallone Era: What It, Uh, All Means," *New York Times,* 22 February 1987, sec. 2, pp. 19, 21.

73. Not long after I wrote this passage, former U.S. Attorney General Ramsey Clark filed 65 claims for compensation with the White House and Defense Department on behalf of civilians killed or injured in the bombing raid. "In the excitement of the news last year and in our love for 'Top Gun' violence and fast jets, we ignore the human pity and suffering that flows [*sic*] from what we do," Clark told reporters. "U.S. asked to pay Libya raid victims," *Poughkeepsie Journal,* 16 April 1987, p. 1A.

*Top Gun,* described by *Time* as "a 110-minute commercial for the Navy," was the highest-grossing film of 1986, earning about $175 million. Its success, predictably, sent studios scrambling to produce war films. In late 1986, the Pentagon was reviewing some 200 screenplays to determine whether it would assist filmmakers with uniforms, tanks, planes, etc. Navy Liaison Officer Sandra Stairs said, "I've seen 10 times more scripts now than in the previous two years." Jacob V. Lamar, Jr., "The Pentagon Goes Hollywood," *Time,* November 24, 1986, p. 30.

74. D.H. Lawrence, *Studies in Classic American Literature* (New York: Viking Press, 1964), p. 62.

# DEATH OF INNOCENCE

> A lot of news is bad news for somebody.... After a while, the somebodies start adding up.—Mac, *Absence of Malice*

THERE HAVE BEEN ANTI-PRESS films nearly as long as there have been "talkies." The most famous and most often remade of all journalism films, *The Front Page* (1931, 1940, 1974, 1988), based on Ben Hecht and Charles MacArthur's 1928 play, is also one of the most cynical about the press.[1] Hildy Johnson, its Odyssean hero who scoops rival reporters by exercising greater cunning and telling bigger, more colorful lies, describes newspaper work with savage scorn: "It's peeking through keyholes. It's running after fire engines, waking up people in the middle of the night to ask them what they thought of Mussolini, and stealing pictures off old ladies after their daughters get attacked in Grove Park. And for what—so a million hired girls and motormen's wives will know what's going on?"

A still darker portrait of journalism emerges from *Five-Star Final* (also 1931). The film was based on a Broadway play by Louis Weitzenkorn, who had worked on the *New York Daily Graphic*, a tabloid more familiarly known as the "Pornographic" for its excessive coverage of sex and violence. Carlos Clarens observed that the film "lingers in the memory as a gangster drama even though no gangsters appear in it."[2] One reason for this is that it stars Edward G. Robinson, whose name is almost synonymous with gangster roles. But a more important reason is that it portrays journalists as vicious and greedy—as gangsters armed with typewriters rather than Tommy guns. Robinson is a managing editor pressured by his publisher, the "sultan of slop," into raking up an ancient scandal in an effort to boost newsstand sales. The result is ruined reputations and a double suicide. In case the viewer somehow missed the point, the final shot of the film shows a copy of the tabloid lying in the gutter and being splattered with slime.

Twenty years later, Billy Wilder's *Ace in the Hole* (retitled *The Big Carnival* when initial box-office returns were poor) depicted the press as willing to go to any lengths for a story. Kirk Douglas played an unprincipled reporter who gets a job on a small New Mexico daily after being banished from big-city journalism. Determined to revive his career with a scoop, he conspires with a corrupt sheriff to delay the rescue of a man trapped in a cave. The story is a six-day sensation. Then the man dies. "[T]he movie," *New York Times* reviewer Nora Sayre said, "is nearly guaranteed to make you hate most reporters."[3]

Desmond Ryan, film critic for the *Philadelphia Inquirer,* was just plain wrong when he wrote that "animosity toward the press in movies—as in real life—is of fairly recent vintage."[4] Far from representing a new negative trend, *Medium Cool* (1969), *Network* (1976), *Absence of Malice* (1981), *The Mean Season* (1984), and other anti-press films of the sixties, seventies, and eighties updated old stereotypes and themes. *Absence of Malice* and *The Mean Season,* for example, each feature an editor who poses as a paternal figure, a mentor and friend of a reporter, but who is actually a Mephistopheles, a corrupter of youth and idealism. *The Front Page* introduced this devious character, in the person of Walter Burns. Burns uses trickery, flattery, and finally physical coercion to keep Hildy Johnson from leaving the paper for marriage and a lucrative job in a New York ad agency. When Malcolm Anderson, the reporter hero of *The Mean Season,* announces his intention to quit daily journalism and go live with his girlfriend in Colorado, his editor, true to type, plays on his vanity and ambition in order to hold him. The eager reporter in *Absence of Malice,* Megan Carter, is likewise manipulated by her editor, Mac, who encourages her in all sorts of unethical behavior. In both the earliest anti-press films and the latest, the editor has been a dark, magnetic presence, seducing and degrading the reporter, an innocent by comparison.

The distinctly modern element in *Absence of Malice* and *The Mean Season* is the seriousness with which the reporters approach their job. In the newspaper films of the thirties and forties, journalism was a big game, and fast-talking reporters played it with a wild competitive spirit, a happy recklessness, gleefully making up the rules as they went along. Their casual attitude toward authority, truth, justice, love—toward everything, really, except scoops—prevented them from developing pompous notions about newspaper work. Regarding the world with a jaundiced eye that had seen the passions and imbecilities flesh is heir to, they accepted that their role was to entertain the public and sell papers, and never fancied themselves the wardens of democracy. Although the reporters in contemporary films are no less competitive and reckless, they lack the cynical self-awareness of their predecessors. They view journalism not as a game or racket, but as a profession, which, ironically, is their greatest mistake and the ultimate cause of their downfall.

Megan and Malcolm live for their work. It is their religion and the basis of their identities. They believe that reporters have an important and clearly defined public mission, sanctioned by the First Amendment, court rulings, and an ideology of professionalism that has been slowly built up over the years. Whipped on by their editors, they assert their professional obligation and legal right to find out and publish whatever they wish, no matter who it hurts. But then something shocking happens that forces them to reassess their absolute devotion to their craft and their brutally literal interpretation of the phrase "freedom of the press." The target of one of Megan's stories commits suicide, while Malcolm's girlfriend is kidnapped by a serial murderer he has been covering and, to some extent, promoting. Suddenly the screen of pretensions and delusions surrounding their prying collapses, and the actual sensational nature of journalism stands thoroughly and damningly revealed. The reporters now realize that saying you were just doing your job is a flimsy excuse for inflicting pain on others, and that professional goals must be restrained by humane values.

Once the protagonists of *Absence of Malice* and *The Mean Season* begin to question the prerogatives of the press, their usefulness to their papers is finished, and they are either driven from journalism or go into self-imposed exile. Megan is fired, and Malcolm departs, at long last, with his girlfriend for Colorado. They had tragically misunderstood their role and pay for it with the death of their innocence. No decision will ever be simple again.

Films critical of TV journalism—*Medium Cool, Network, Wrong Is Right* (1981), and *Power* (1986)—don't follow so unified and recognizable a formula as those about print journalism. Rather than sharing a particular story pattern, they share an anxious, chaotic atmosphere. Random violence abounds, and in *Medium Cool* and *Network,* claims the heroes for victims. *Wrong is Right* opens with correspondent Patrick Hale reporting from the Happy Farm, where, for $400, "you can safely work out your fantasies of violence" (killing parents is the most popular). "Is violence becoming a national pastime?" he portentously asks. "Is it as American as apple pie?" All the films suggest that it is, and that TV is pretty much to blame. In *Medium Cool,* cameraman John Cassellis, watching a TV documentary on the assassinations of John and Robert Kennedy and Martin Luther King, Jr., holds out his hands toward the glowing set and says: "Feel it? X rays? Is that what it is? Does it grow hair? Is it vitamins? Can you feel violence?" TV is a fearsome new force, controlled by soulless corporations, yet bowed down to like a god by the public. How fittingly ironic that in *Network* a large, stained-glass disc hangs from the rafters of the TV studio in parody of a cathedral.

Decades before the invention of either TV or the movies, novelists, among others, were already expressing dread that the semiliterate masses would fall prey to ruthless press lords. David Graham Phillips' *The Great God Success* (1901) and William Richard Hereford's *The Demagog* (1909) reflected the status panic and moral outrage that were unleashed by the revolutionary changes then sweeping journalism, from mechanization and the rise of sensational mass-circulation dailies to the growth of newspaper monopolies. Phillips' and Hereford's protagonists are publishers of yellow journals who, behind their proud pose as crusaders, use their papers to shape public opinion for their own base ends.

If there were ever a figure meant for the big screen, the conniving media mogul, with his grand style and vast appetite for money and power, may have been it. D.B. Norton (Edward Arnold) in Frank Capra's *Meet John Doe* (1941) was an early film version of this shark in a silk suit. Backed by a cabal of business and labor leaders, Norton pursues a secret plan to set himself up as dictator of the United States, and thanks to the propaganda spewed out by his nationwide network of newspapers and radio stations, he very nearly succeeds. His kind has since personified vanity and greed in a host of other films. Even Sam Fuller's *Park Row* (1952), a sentimental tribute to turn-of-the-century journalism in New York, includes a portrait of a power-mad publisher and the warning refrain, "The press is good or evil according to the character of those who direct it." These movies, like their literary forerunners, betray a deep and abiding fear of the incipient mob that lurks within the democratic populace, a mob that the shivarees of the mass media threaten to arouse.

Today's anti-press films are no less galling to journalists for having numerous precedents. Former editor Norman Isaacs noted that the "most sacred cow in journalism's holy credo [is] its self-proclaimed right to reject any type of examination of its performance."[5] Journalists tend to react to criticism not as if they have thin skin, but as if they have no skin. In their hypersensitive state, every remark against the press seems a potentially disastrous crack in the ramparts of the First Amendment. "I sometimes think," David Shaw, media reporter for the *Los Angeles Times,* said, "that the phrase 'chilling effect'—as in 'This will have a "chilling effect" on the ability of the press to fulfill its First Amendment obligations'—is routinely administered to all journalists, by injection, with their first press cards."[6] Journalism is in the ironic position of claiming the right to scrutinize others while resenting scrutiny of itself.

Such obvious arrogance may be "one of the root causes of the huge loss of journalism's credibility with its audiences."[7] Reporters and editors conceive of themselves as professionals, possessing rights and privileges the rest of us don't. As James Carey explained, the professions "insist that each inhabits a particular moral universe, peculiar unto itself, in which the standards and judgments exercised are those not of the general society and its moral point of view, but a distinctive code."[8] News people justify their conduct, when they deign to justify it at all, by spouting slogans that they have inflated into immutable principles—confidentiality of sources, for example, or the public's right to know. The problem is that broad segments of society have refused to be bound by the special claims of the press. Robert W. Greene, assistant managing editor of *Newsday,* put it bluntly: "We are more and more appearing as some sort of privileged class. The public despises privileged classes."[9]

One doesn't have to look too hard to find signs of just how much the public despises the press:

- Of the 106 major libel cases that reached juries between 1976 and 1984, journalists lost 90, and almost a quarter of the damage awards were $1 million or more.[10]

- When U.S. forces attacked the Caribbean island of Grenada in 1983, the Reagan administration banned reporters from the scene for the first 48 hours of the invasion. Journalists protested the news blackout, but the public enthusiastically approved it. *Editor & Publisher,* in an informal survey of about a dozen dailies, found letters to the editor were running three to one in favor of the ban.[11]

- In 1986 then-CIA director William Casey voiced dismay at "the propensity of the American press to publish classified information, which destroys and jeopardizes intelligence sources and methods." He asked the Justice Department to consider prosecuting the *Washington Post* under an espionage law dating back to the Cold War era if the newspaper reported the details of a spy case. The move, which one writer characterized as the "harshest confrontation between the government and the press since the publication of the Pentagon Papers" in 1971, sparked no public outcry.[12]

• At about the same time, NBC News filmed an exclusive interview with Palestinian terrorist leader Abul Abbas after agreeing not to disclose his whereabouts. In the interview, Abbas threatened President Reagan and the American people. Viewers were appalled. One said in a letter to *Time* magazine: "The press has the responsibility to distinguish between covering news and creating news that will serve the self-interests of certain groups. Giving terrorists the notoriety they thrive on is like feeding the mouth that bites you."[13]

Under fire from all sides, journalists have resorted to frequent credibility studies to reassure themselves that they aren't as universally distrusted as they seem to be. The polls are a convenient and relatively inexpensive substitute for internal reform. *Columbia Journalism Review* wondered in a recent editorial why the press was so infatuated with such surveys and concluded, "Perhaps credibility is a less demanding standard than accuracy or comprehensiveness."[14]

A 1985 Gallup poll was the "largest, most fully integrated analysis ever conducted into public thinking about the American news media."[15] Titled "The People & The Press," it was commissioned by Times Mirror, the corporation that owns the *Los Angeles Times, Newsday,* five other papers, five magazines, four TV stations, and 50 cable systems. (In a curious lapse, respondents weren't asked their opinion about media monopolies.) Overall, the statistics cited in the survey, or at least the interpretations

Gallup gave them, reinforced the journalistic status quo. Eight-two to 87 percent of the sample rated national news organizations as either "believable" or "highly believable."[16] The pollster stoutly declared, "There is no credibility crisis for the nation's news media."[17]

Times Mirror, in a mood of self-congratulation, launched a series of full-page ads in newspapers and magazines ballyhooing the results of the study. This may have been good public relations, but good public relations may not be all that is needed. For tucked among the survey's more positive findings were hints of widespread disenchantment with press performance. Seventy-three percent of the respondents believed that reporters invade people's privacy; 60 percent saw journalists as too interested in bad news; and 55 percent said news organizations are likely to try and cover up their mistakes.[18]

And there was more. Fifty-three percent regarded the press "*not* as independent." Heavy majorities felt that the news is often influenced by the federal government (78 percent), big business (70 percent), advertisers (65 percent), and labor unions (62 percent).[19] The impression among the respondents was that journalists are, as someone once said, cheerleaders for the side that has already won.

What will news organizations do with these alarming findings? Not much, probably. It will be business as usual, because the media business is unusually profitable. According to *Advertising Age,* 12 of 1984's top 100 media companies had revenues exceeding a billion dollars each. The total income of the 100 companies was $50.2 billion, an increase of 19.1 percent from 1983.[20] Rolling in money, the press has no real incentive to heed the warning signs and act more responsibly.

Anti-press films give the public a chance to vent their frustration with a press that has grown imperious and remote. In some of the films—*Absence of Malice* and *The Mean Season* immediately spring to mind—an incompetent or overaggressive reporter is the apparent focus of criticism. Yet there is also a semiarticulate awareness in these films that reporters and frontline editors are victims of their jobs, men and women caught in a complex web of institutional pressures. As investigative journalist Robert Sherrill pointed out, even if you could help most reporters by sending them to an ethics training camp, the odds against improving the media would still be hefty. "The reason," he said, "is that most of the really significant crumminess in journalism is not at the bottom but at the very top."[21]

Films about broadcast journalism explicitly share that view, taking network and local station owners to task for what J. Edward Murray called the "profit response to the First Amendment." He was referring to how the media, and TV in particular, bastardize and trivialize the news to attract bigger audiences.[22] *Network* and *Wrong Is Right* associate TV news with the ripest kinds of sensationalism—tits, blood, disease, madness, death. Both films exaggerate, though perhaps no worse than TV does. The typical TV news show, with its dramatic "live" reports, flashy computer graphics, blow-dried anchors, and opening and closing music, has hopelessly blurred the line between information and entertainment. Its godfather isn't Zenger, but Ziegfeld. "The result of all this," Neil Postman of New York University claimed, "is that Americans are the best-entertained and likely the least well-informed people in the Western world."[23]

Print journalists routinely blame TV for the low esteem in which the public holds the press. TV lets people see reporters in action, and the sight of the journalistic pack closing in on a government official or yapping at grieving relatives after a tragedy offends many. Ben Bradlee, executive editor of the *Washington Post,* said, "Television has changed the public's vision of the reporter into someone who is petty and disagreeable and who has taken cynicism the unnecessary extra steps."[24] It has done a lot more than that; it has fundamentally changed the way the public stays informed. Over the past 25 years, TV has become the main source of information for upwards of 60 percent of Americans. They get from it their politics, their religion, their lifestyles. "Right now television has culture by its throat. . . . ," Postman lamented.[25] Such tyranny has proved a tempting target for anyone with a rock handy.

It is supremely hypocritical, of course, for Hollywood to belabor the press for giving people the sort of sensational and trivial stuff they seem to want. Hollywood itself makes and markets movies based on demographics and has long understood and exploited the box-office appeal of sex, crime, and violence. "[T]he perennial Hollywood question . . . ," film scholar Gerald Weales wrote, "was never 'Is it art?' but 'Will it sell?' "[26] Ironically, when filmmakers indict journalism for perverting reality for the sake of profits, they are indicting their own motives and methods, too.

The latest cycle of anti-press films is an example of the snake swallowing its tail in another regard. Those who control the entertainment industry and those who control the news business are, increasingly, one and the same group. Tabloid publisher Rupert Murdoch, a real-life sultan of slop, spent $1.6 billion in 1984-85 to acquire 12 trade magazines from Ziff-Davis, six independent TV stations from Metromedia, Inc., and sole ownership of 20th Century-Fox Film Corporation.[27] Ted Turner, head of the Turner Broadcasting System, which includes the Cable News Network, failed in his effort to take over CBS, but bought MGM/UA Entertainment Company for $1.5 billion. In March 1986, six months after the deal was consummated, Turner said of the media industry, "It is a business where the big are getting bigger, and the small are disappearing."[28]

Today the ownerships of newspapers, magazines, book companies, radio and TV stations, and film studios are constantly shifting in a frantic financial game of musical chairs. Karen Rothmeyer, a contributing editor to the *Columbia Journalism Review,* wrote that "the current media-acquisition craze has been largely fueled by the simple desire to make a bundle."[29] Or maybe not so simple, for it has revived worries about concentrated media power being used to intimidate, to propagandize, to drown out a diversity of voices with a "bottom-line, dollar-sign chorus" of corporate voices.[30] The fear that the press is becoming the publicity arm of big business has found its way into journalism films, with the strange result that the investors and bankers behind the films are sometimes the very people the films warn us about.

Rothmeyer asserted that the frenzied trading in media companies threatens "many journalists' image of themselves as a breed set apart from the crass world of commerce."[31] Yet, if this were really the case, editorial workers would probably be more vocal in their opposition to the buying and selling of newspapers and broadcast properties. "As long as the new owners don't change salaries or benefits most employees don't care," said the general manager of a Midwest TV station that was sold twice in two years.[32] Journalists evidently see a greater threat to their professional status emanating from Hollywood screening rooms than from Wall Street board rooms. Which is why they hardly ever take loud exception to media mergers, but often object strenuously to journalism films.

No film of the eighties so consternated and angered journalists as *Absence of Malice.* It is the story of a young, misguided reporter and her scoop-hungry editor, who, in their rush to publish, ravage innocent people. Robert Hatch told readers of *The Nation,* "The film's basic premise is that a successful newspaper can be run by irresponsible fools, a notion that will strike thoughtful viewers as improbable. Unfortunately," he added, "not all viewers are thoughtful...."[33] Pulitzer Prize-winning reporter Lucinda Franks described the journalists in the film as "grotesquely distorted." She found their reckless behavior "astonishing not for its unethicality, but for its stupidity."[34] Echoes of the original controversy over *Absence of Malice* were still being heard four years after the movie's release. "More than any other film, it demonstrates the difference between what reporters do on the street and what they are shown doing on the screen," Desmond Ryan wrote in a 1985 article.[35]

The attacks on *Absence of Malice* stemmed from paranoia on the part of journalists that the film would feed public discontent with the news media. Hatch, in his January 1982 review, wished that the movie wasn't playing in theaters just then.[36] Journalism had recently suffered through a series of embarrassments and imbroglios. TV coverage of the takeover of the U.S. embassy in Tehran by

Iranian militants and the reporting of the FBI's Abscam investigation ("Justice by press release," the director of the American Civil Liberties Union had called it) had raised eyebrows.[37] So had the Janet Cooke hoax and the *Washington Post*'s front-page apology to President Carter for implying in a gossip column that he had bugged Blair House while the Reagans were staying there before inauguration day. Such miscues seemed to lend credence to *Absence of Malice.* Moreover, the $13-million film had verisimilitude. Some of the newsroom scenes were shot at the *Miami Herald,* "which by now," Hatch wryly noted, "probably regrets its hospitality."[38] Jonathan Friendly of the *New York Times* pointed out that the movie was "filled with small touches—the computer terminals on the reporters' desks, the roaring presses, the paperboy on his bike—designed to suggest that it is presenting the reality of newspapering."[39] What most alarmed journalists about the film was that, coming when it did, audiences might accept its negative portrayal of their profession at face value.

They also were shocked at the swiftness and completeness of their fall from public grace, at least as measured by Hollywood movies. Sidney Pollack, director of *Absence of Malice,* had earlier made *Three Days of the Condor* (1975), in which Robert Redford, on the run from a malevolent CIA, turns for safety to the *New York Times.* The following year Alan Pakula's *All the President's Men* had glamorized the two young reporters who had broken the Watergate story and helped bring down a president. Now, in less than a decade, the press was back in the doghouse. *Time* magazine's Richard Schickel claimed, "*Absence of Malice* does not invalidate *All the President's Men,*" but that wasn't how most journalists saw it.[40] Speaking for the majority, Franks protested that the film "aims to take away our last bone of glory."[41]

Many journalists weren't only convinced that *Absence of Malice* was a hatchet job; they were convinced that the hatchet belonged to the screenwriter. Although Franks said one might argue that movies mirror "what is on society's mind at a particular point in time," and that therefore "*Absence of Malice* is letting us know that the public is angry," she herself wasn't inclined to make that argument. She much preferred to emphasize the obvious: "[T]he 'public' didn't write the script; it was written by Kurt Luedtke, former executive editor of the *Detroit Free Press*."[42] Luedtke was a journalist of 20 years' experience when, in 1979, he went to try his hand in Hollywood (he would win a 1985 Oscar for his literate script for another Pollack movie, *Out of Africa*). In the furor over *Absence of Malice,* he was judged a traitor to his old profession, a curious verdict in light of the fact that ex-newspapermen had been writing journalism films since the days of Hecht and MacArthur. Given their low pay, long hours, and shaky status, journalists have always had plenty of cause for complaint about newspaper life. But they generally complain out of earshot of the public, while sitting around the newsroom on slow nights or in a bar after the paper has been put to bed. Luedtke's offense was that he aired the press' self-doubts in front of strangers, millions of them.

Naturally, he denied doing anything of the kind. He insisted in a *New York Times* interview that the film wasn't meant as a description of how the press usually operates. If audiences take it for that, he said, "then indeed, it's unfair, in that it doesn't show a number of the very good, very healthy things that the press does every day. I hope nobody takes it that way." And he thought that nobody would. In his words, "I don't walk out of a bad-cop movie saying what I have been told is that the police are bad people."[43] Yet elsewhere both Luedtke and Pollack defended *Absence of Malice* from the slings and arrows of outraged journalists by maintaining that the incidents of unethical reporting in it had real-life counterparts.[44]

Consider a scene at the beginning of the film in which Megan Carter (Sally Field), reporter for the *Miami Standard,* sneaks a look at a file that the head of a federal strike force has left lying on his desk. She thinks that she is outsmarting the FBI agent, but actually she is falling into his trap. He put the file there to trick Megan into believing that Michael Gallagher (Paul Newman), an honest liquor wholesaler who also happens to be the son and nephew of mobsters, is a suspect in the disappearance of a union boss.

The idea behind the ploy is that newspaper publicity will pressure Gallagher into telling what he presumably knows about the crime. Precisely as the agent calculated, Megan writes a front-page story without checking with other sources or bothering to get a response from Gallagher. She thus sets in motion a long, complex chain of events that will lead through shattered reputations and a suicide to her own firing.

Reviewers found it scarcely credible that a reporter would base a story on a single source—and that, a clearly tainted one.[45] But incredible as this particular action may be, the overall scene makes a legitimate point about the too common failure of journalists to look beyond the surface in their eagerness for a big scoop. The Janet Cooke fiasco has been ascribed to the gullibility of her editors at the *Washington Post,* who saw in the fake about a child heroin addict what they wanted to see—a "helluva story," a Pulitzer Prize—and ignored the flashing caution lights.[46] A more recent example of journalistic wishful thinking involved both NBC and ABC. A day after the explosion at the Chernobyl nuclear-power plant in central Russia in April 1986, the two networks broadcast footage of what was allegedly the damaged plant. The pictures, for which they jointly paid a Rome photo agency $2,000, turned out to be of a cement factory in Trieste, Italy. Here was another instance where a little of the press's legendary skepticism might have gone a long way.

So far as I am aware, no reviewers complained that Megan's picking up the FBI file was unrealistic. Quite the contrary. Franks said many real-life reporters would have done the same. "Press ethics are, at best, elastic," she observed.[47] But a major theme of *Absence of Malice* is that when journalists stretch ethics, innocent people can get hurt in the snapback.

Norman Isaacs has written that ethics "consists of knowing right from wrong, and following a right course as an honorable duty."[48] Most often, however, the news media use legal, not ethical, criteria in deciding whose privacy to invade and how far to go. The *Standard*'s lawyer assures Megan that the paper can safely publish the Gallagher story; whether it is right to do so is never discussed. Sanctimoniously, he invokes a series of Supreme Court rulings that have held that public officials or figures must prove actual malice or reckless disregard of the truth to sustain a libel suit. "We have no knowledge your story is false," explains the lawyer, putting in his thumb and pulling out a plum of a defense, "therefore we are absent malice. We have been both reasonable and prudent, therefore we are not negligent. We may say what we like about Mr. Gallagher and he is powerless to do us harm. Democracy is served."

It is Gallagher's powerlessness, his inability to get a fair hearing from the paper, that provides the dramatic and moral center of the film. After the story identifying him as a suspect runs, he confronts Megan in the newsroom. Flustered, she knocks over a cup of coffee on her desk. She has suddenly been reminded, as she will be several more times, that she is writing about people who bleed if cut, something easy to forget when bent over a computer keyboard, racing a deadline. "I want to know

Liquor wholesaler Michael Gallagher (Paul Newman), the innocent victim of anonymous sources and scoop-hungry journalists, confronts reporter Megan Carter (Sally Field) in *Absence of Malice.*

where this story came from," Gallagher says, but the paper isn't talking. His plight calls into question journalism's dependence on secret sources, suggesting that it is contrary to the American system of justice, under which the accused is entitled to face his accusers. The press may style itself the guardian of civil liberties, but it is portrayed as an accomplice in Star Chamber proceedings.

Later Gallagher has lunch with Megan and tries to give his side of the story. She wears a tape-recorder microphone disguised as a stickpin for the occasion, and a photographer in a Volkswagen lurks in the background. Gallagher, who is shrewder than either the *Standard* or the FBI recognizes, asks, "What else do you want to know?"

> **Megan:** "Whatever you want to tell me. Look, I really want to be fair about this."
>
> **Gallagher:** "One of those upfront ladies."
>
> **Megan:** "I try to be."
>
> **Gallagher:** "Who's the guy in the Volkswagen?" [He grabs her lapel.] "And who the hell am I talking to?"
>
> **Megan:** "Oh shit. . . . Gallagher, I'm a reporter. What did you expect? Don't try to make me feel guilty."
>
> **Gallagher:** "Somebody is trying to get to me, somebody with no face and no name. You're the gofer. You listen to them, you write what they say, and you help them hide. . . . "
>
> **Megan:** "If they clear you, we'll print it."
>
> **Gallagher:** "What page? See, you say somebody's guilty, people believe it. You say they're not guilty, nobody's interested."
>
> **Megan:** "That's not the paper's fault. It's people. People believe what they want to believe."
>
> **Gallagher:** "Who puts out the paper? Nobody?"

The journalists in the film do act almost as if nobody puts out the paper. Whenever they are forced to justify or explain their role, they voice the "assumptions of laissez-faire liberalism."[49] They conceive of the press as a neutral agency, a kind of giant switchboard for relaying messages. How the public treats the messages isn't their concern. "We just tell the truth," Megan's editor, Mac (Josef Sommer), smugly says. "Let other people decide what's right." But news and truth aren't synonymous. An accurately quoted lie is still a lie. At one point, Gallagher cautions Megan: "You don't write the truth. You write what people say.... You don't come across the truth that easy." *Absence of Malice* takes the position that the proclaimed objectivity of the press is a cover for carelessness and self-interest. It is all to their own advantage for Megan and Mac to assume that they aren't responsible for the consequences of the stories they print, that their moral obligation ends well short of where the pain the stories inflict begins.

For Gallagher, the pain is intense. As a result of Megan's stories his business is shut down and a lifelong friend, Teresa Perrone (Melinda Dillion), is destroyed. A young woman on the brink of nervous collapse, Teresa has evidence that will clear Gallagher, but that also will scandalize her co-workers at a Catholic school and her family. Megan brushes aside her pleas for privacy—"I'm a reporter. You're talking to a newspaper right now."—and proceeds to extract an intimate confession from her. It emerges that Gallagher was with Teresa in Atlanta when the labor leader disappeared. She remembers the date because she was having an abortion. "That's not such a terrible thing.... People will understand," Megan says, and dashes back to the office to write the scoop. Early the next morning, Teresa goes from house to house on the street where she lives, gathering the just-delivered papers so her neighbors won't learn her secret. She is crazy with fear and shame, and, soon after, kills herself.

The suicide hits Megan hard. Mac, the chief spokesman in the film for journalistic values, tries to console her: "Look, people get caught up in things. Remember the woman in San Francisco a few years ago took a shot at Ford, and there was a guy in the crowd grabbed her arm and saved the president's life, and he was a hero? It turned out that he also was gay. It was news, right? Now the whole country knows."

> **Megan:** "Did he kill himself?"
>
> **Mac:** "It was not your fault."

But appeals to "the public's right to know" and other big, abstract principles can never excuse the brutal reality of Teresa's death. "Couldn't you see what it was to her?" Gallagher snarls at Megan. "Couldn't you just stop scribbling for a second, just put down your goddamn ballpoint pen, and just see her?" In his anger, he hurls the reporter to the floor, tearing her clothes. Some of the elements of a rape—the empty warehouse, the animal savagery, the naked white flesh—are present in the scene. The film symbolically invites the audience, which by now fully identifies with Gallagher, to join in the assault, to stick it back to the press that has been sticking it to them for so long.

On a more conscious level, the film permits the audience a sweet revenge by having Gallagher concoct a plan in which his tormentors' own eagerness is employed to trip them up. He is cleared, the FBI is embarrassed, and Megan is fired. Ordinary people don't usually get to even the score with the press, but, of course, that is why they manage to do so in the movies. If movies just showed life, no one would pay to see them.

*Absence of Malice* grows fainthearted at the last minute and tries to withdraw the harsh things it has been saying about routine journalistic practices for two hours. Megan tells Gallagher: "I know that you think what I do for a living is nothing. It really isn't nothing. I just did it badly." But the press isn't cured of its blindness and arrogance now that Megan is out of a job. The paper that encouraged her irresponsibility is still there and still clinging to flawed notions of objectivity and truth. Another reporter, a younger, taller, blonder version of Megan, takes over the

Gallagher story, and with it, all of the narrow professional habits of mind. The torch has been passed to a new generation, and they will probably burn down the house.

Director Phillip Borsos' *The Mean Season* (1985) covers a lot of the same ground as *Absence of Malice*. The film is based on John Katzenbach's novel, *In the Heat of the Summer,* which itself was inspired by the highly publicized correspondence between the "Son of Sam" killer and *New York Daily News* columnist Jimmy Breslin. Like *Absence of Malice,* it examines the tangled reporter-source relationship, but gives the relationship an even harder twist by making the source a serial murderer. Also like *Absence of Malice,* it is set in Miami, though not the pretty Miami of picture postcards. The action takes place during hurricane season, when the sky rumbles and flashes, and a hot wind blows. Borsos uses the steamy Florida background as a metaphor for the complex corruption of the film's reporter hero.

The makers of *The Mean Season* took pains to re-create the gritty atmosphere of a big-city daily. Katzenbach, a veteran crime reporter who declined to write the screenplay but who was a helper on the set, said, "If there wasn't a sense of verisimilitude, the people in the profession would jump all over [the film].... the one group of people I didn't want to rise up en masse were my contemporaries."[50] The newsroom scenes were shot at the *Miami Herald* in the middle of the night, to pre-recorded soundtracks of the paper's staff locked in noisy battle with afternoon deadlines. "I'm a nut for detail," confessed producer David Foster, a graduate of the journalism school at the University of Southern California. "That's what makes a film look the way it looks and behave the way it behaves."[51] Foster sat in on "budget" meetings, where editors allocate space and decide which stories go on the front page. Kurt Russell, who stars as reporter Malcolm Anderson, accompanied a *Herald* reporter and photographer on assignments. Richard Masur prepared for his role as Bill Nolan, Malcolm's hard-nosed editor, by spending time on the *Herald*'s city desk.[52]

Most reviewers felt that the efforts paid off. Vincent Canby of the *New York Times* wrote, "...'The Mean Season' is awfully good at depicting the routine of the fictional Miami Journal . . . , the crises and tensions of daily journalism, the sense of life being lived in 24-hour installments."[53] Yet the film, for all its attention to surface detail, derives its iconography less from newspaper life than from early newspaper movies. The opening sequence showing the presses thundering away and freshly printed papers being cut, folded, and bundled places *The Mean Season* squarely within the strictures and stereotypes of the journalism film genre. And the borrowing doesn't stop there. Borsos resorts to the decrepit device of superimposing front pages on scenes—mercifully, the pages don't spin into view—to condense the action. If the visual clichés were intended ironically (the case with another film of the same year, *Not for Publication*), they might be excused or even applauded. Unfortunately, the director gives no sign of having his tongue in his cheek, only stale ideas in his head.

*The Mean Season* still manages to raise pertinent questions about journalism ethics. At the start of the film, Malcolm is a victim of burnout, a newsroom malady resulting from stress and long hours and from covering too many sad and sordid crimes. "I don't want to see my name in the paper next to pictures of dead bodies anymore," he says. He is planning to leave the *Journal* and go off with his girlfriend, schoolteacher Christine Connelly (Mariel Hemingway), to Colorado, where he will edit a sleepy, small-town weekly and heal his emotional wounds. Nolan, who doesn't want to lose his star reporter, tries to hold Malcolm with glib rationalizations for the way journalists swoop down like vultures on stories of violence and bloodshed. "[W]e're not the manufacturers," the editor explains, "we just retail. News gets made somewhere else, we just sell it."

Whether the press simply reports the news or participates in it is tested when Malcolm begins getting phone calls from the "Numbers Killer" (Richard Jordan). "Look, you're going to be my conduit to the public," the murderer says. The *Journal* decides to cooperate with the headline-hungry maniac for a variety of reasons, all of them dubious. At the meeting where the decision is taken, Malcolm waves the tattered old banner of the public's right to know: "I think we have the chance here, let alone the obligation, to do a piece on a sociopath who's still out there.... That's our responsibility, isn't it?" Nolan makes a cruder, but perhaps more persuasive, appeal. "This story is going to sell a hell of a lot of newspapers for somebody," he notes. The publisher is chiefly concerned about the potential for costly libel suits. "Legally," he asks the paper's lawyers, "how far could our asses be hanging out?" Assured that their asses are protected, the journalists plunge ahead with the story. In *The Mean Season,* as in *Absence of Malice,* the press puts legality before justice, and economics before ethics.

The movie basically argues that the *Journal* encourages the killer by publicizing his gory deeds. "It's turned into a collaboration," Christine says as the death count rises and the front-page headliners grow bigger and more sensational. The killer himself tells Malcolm, "We work well together." For most of the picture, they share the same warped perspective, the same darkness of the soul. Both need an audience and both claim to be somehow beyond ordinary morality. "I'm not responsible, it's not my fault," the killer declares at one point, echoing an assertion by Malcolm that "Things happen out there. It's called news. I only report it." Malcolm, however, doesn't just cover the murders; he develops a stake in their continuing. Because of his exclusive relationship with the killer, he captures national media attention and is flattered to be invited on network TV shows and written up in *Time.* His ambition and ego also are fed by Nolan, who calculatedly remarks, "Our illustrious publisher thinks you may be entering Pulitzer territory." It was journalists of Malcolm's type that Lyle Denniston, Supreme Court reporter for the *Baltimore Sun,* had in mind when he said: "The power-groupie, the fame-driven person runs through this profession now in great numbers. I don't think people respect truth very much: they respect theater and they respect excitement, but truth isn't a driving proposition anymore."[54]

As fate—or, rather, the screenwriters—would have it,

Malcolm Anderson (Kurt Russell) exchanges his computer terminal for a gun in *The Mean Season,* while his girlfriend (Mariel Hemingway) screams hysterically in the background.

the killer becomes jealous of Malcolm's sudden stardom. "I do all the work and you get put on TV," he huffs. To cut the reporter back down to size, he poses as a source having information about the killer's identity. Malcolm follows in the footsteps of Megan Carter and rushes into print without attempting to verify the story. Once again, lust for a scoop is shown ravaging the diligent search for truth. The story no sooner appears than it is exposed as a hoax and must be retracted. While struggling with the wording of the correction, Nolan says to Malcolm, "You're going to take a public whipping like no one's ever seen."

But viewers demand something more in the way of atonement, and so the killer kidnaps Christine. The terror Malcolm helped unleash now invades his own life. He personally suffers, yet having suffered, is reborn as a superhero, in one instance even leaping across an opening drawbridge. The plot, after several more twists and turns, finally brings the reporter and the killer together for an apocalyptic confrontation. Malcolm wrestles the gun from the psychopath and fires, slaying his evil twin, his shadow self. And the gun blast has another, and broader, effect. It renders moot the ethical questions raised earlier by the film. In the midst of Malcolm's obsessive involvement with the killer, Christine had warned him, "When this thing is over, whether you end up at a 20-cent weekly or the *New York Times,* part of it stays with you." She was wrong. The film suggests that no problem is too complex, no situation too ambiguous, no past too long and tangled, that it can't be resolved by a well-aimed bullet.

Although *The Mean Season* grants Malcolm a blanket pardon, the rest of journalism stands convicted of irresponsibility and heartlessness. Punctuating the film are wild scenes of reporters and TV crews intruding on people at their moments of greatest anguish. "Nothing like blood, shit, and hot weather to bring out the flies," a detective says as journalists buzz around the parents of a young murder victim. After the film is over, and despite its happy ending, what stays with you is the cruelty of the press.

Sharp as the attack on newspaperdom is in contemporary movies, the attack on TV journalism is even sharper. In such films as *Medium Cool, Network,* and *Wrong Is Right,* TV reporters have all the faults of their print brethren, plus a few new ones of their own. The popularity of an art form or entertainment medium has always been enough to condemn it in some eyes, and TV, as John M. Phelan wrote, is "the most mass of the media."[55] Ninety million Americans tune in every night.[56] There are more TV sets in the United States than telephones or toilets.[57] Underlying the Hollywood portrayal of TV journalism is the assumption that the larger the audience, the larger the temptation and opportunity for psychological manipulation and political control.

Over the past quarter century, TV has, in fact, irradiated American culture with its ghostly blue light. It has driven powerful pictures into our heads: of slain President Kennedy lying in state beneath the Capitol dome; of

Iranian militants, their fists raised, chanting "Death to America" outside the U.S. embassy in Tehran; of the space shuttle Challenger exploding in a fireball. But by the same process of reiteration, it also had driven noise and nonsense into our heads and scrambled our sense of reality. With a gigantic audience of unequal education and uncertain understanding to enthrall, TV has degraded public discourse, reducing complicated issues and ideas to the level of situation comedies and advertising slogans. We devour TV images and, in turn, are devoured by them. We take our cues for how to live from commercials and talk shows and soap operas. We search for our lost youth among endless reruns. A "vast wasteland," to borrow the phrase Newton N. Minow, former chairman of the Federal Communications Commission, used to describe TV programming, has become our home.[58]

All of big-time journalism is governed by the profit motive, but TV journalism seems particularly so. Unlike the American newspaper, whose origins antedate the rise of modern advertising by two centuries, TV was "conceived, born, and developed as a selling medium."[59] What it sells are audiences to advertisers. The more viewers a program attracts, the more advertisers can be charged. A single ratings point represents millions of dollars. As a result, broadcasters are locked in relentless competition for the highest possible ratings. TV journalists have been inexorably drawn into the battle. "It's trench warfare," Van Gordon Sauter, recent president of CBS News, said. "There's everything out there but mustard gas."[60]

Hoping to expand their share of the audience, station owners and managers have looked to market research to resolve doubts about what to put on the air. Outside consultants, or "show doctors," most of whom have little journalistic experience, have been summoned to prescribe for ailing news programs.[61] Their advice, based on opinion surveys, has wreaked havoc on traditional standards of editorial excellence. It has eroded the distinction between information and entertainment, leading to a strange hybrid called "infotainment." Local news directors now speak of striving to create "a theater of information, an upbeat show," and of wanting to "make people simmer in their seats when they watch us."[62] Entertainment values have even invaded the once sacred grove of the network evening news, as is illustrated by the star salaries paid the anchors: Dan Rather of CBS earns about $2.5 million a year; Tom Brokaw of NBC, about $1.8 million; and Peter Jennings of ABC, about $900,000.[63] The implication is that the person who presents the news is more important than the news he presents.

In the crassly commercial atmosphere of TV journalism, the public is treated not as citizens to be enlightened, but as consumers to be enticed. There is an inclination to play on people's morbid curiosity, their fantasies and fears. An NBC producer has remarked, only half-jokingly, that the ideal teaser for a feature story would go like this: "Rape, pillage, and destruction. Details at eleven."[64]

The sophisticated hardware introduced within the past decade—computers, communication satellites, the mobile Minicam—has merely aggravated the tendency toward trivia and sensation. It was recognized as far back as the 1840s, at least by the perspicacious few, that technological advances don't necessarily translate into moral or cultural progress. "We are in great haste to construct a magnetic telegraph from Maine to Texas," Henry David Thoreau wrote in *Walden,* "but Maine and Texas, it may be, having nothing important to communicate.... We are eager to tunnel under the Atlantic and bring the old world some weeks nearer to the new, but perchance the first news that will leak through into the broad flapping American ear will be that Princess Adelaide has the whooping cough."[65] Similarly, if more recently, Burton Benjamin, who was executive producer of "CBS Evening News With Walter Cronkite," said: "I am not certain that creativity in television news is keeping up with the technology. Do we do all of these dazzling things—flood the screen with whirling images, go live, cover non-events thousands of miles away—just so we can say You Are There?"[66] Hell, yes. Bob Teague, veteran correspondent for WNBC-TV in New York, complained that the Minicam, a lightweight camera that can be plugged into a microwave dish atop a van for live reporting, is often used solely because it permits news directors to flash the magic word "Live" on the screen. With depressing frequency, audiences are now subjected to a "live spot from the field that shows nothing of significance: just a reporter surrounded by gawkers and 'Hi-Mom' wavers, talking about something that either happened three hours ago or might happen an hour later."[67]

Even when there is important news to tell, TV may be incapable of telling it coherently. A half-hour news program is too short (22 minutes of news and eight minutes of commercials) to afford more than a surface view of events; the total words on a network newscast would fill about half of a typical newspaper page. In addition, the format is rigidly stylized, from the heartrending interviews with stunned disaster victims to the lighthearted final story. Then, also, the information goes by at lightning speed. "One of the chief challenges of television," Edwin Diamond commented, "has always been to make events understandable through a medium—spoken words accompanying moving pictures—that is superb for conveying emotion but practically opaque for the transmission of sustained thought."[68] Research by Mark R. Levy and John P. Robinson of the University of Maryland has revealed that "the average viewer fails to understand the main points in two-thirds of all major TV news stories." They concluded that "people who watch TV news are only slightly better informed than people who don't, and other things being equal, people who say TV is their main source for news are among the least-informed members of the public."[69] There is exceptional danger in a society like ours, saturated with TV images that bewilder and mislead, of democratic processes breaking down. As James Madison prophetically warned, "A popular government without popular information, or the means of acquiring it, is but a Prologue to a Farce or a Tragedy; or perhaps both."[70]

The conventional definition of news as the current, the dramatic, the extraordinary further diminishes the value of most TV journalism. TV demands pictures, and the bloodier, the better, because the more likely to arrest attention. Now an earthquake, next a car bomb, and when we return, a murder-suicide. The world of TV news is a world in flames. Viewers are hammered by what Christopher Lasch called the "propaganda of death and destruction"—with time out, of course, for commercials, sports, weather, and banter among the anchors.[71] Newscasts may produce the illusion of informing, but instead of disclosing a meaningful pattern among events, they promote fragmentation and incoherence, spraying the audience with disconnected images and echoes, electronic shrapnel. Neil Postman went so far as to say that "embedded in the surrealistic frame of a television news show is a theory of anticommunication, featuring a type of discourse that abandons logic, reason, sequence and rules of contradiction. In aesthetics, I believe the name given to this theory is Dadaism; in philosophy, nihilism; in psychiatry, schizophrenia. In the parlance of the theater, it is known as vaudeville."[72]

Films that condemn TV news for competitiveness, sensationalism, and superficiality also condemn the mass audience that watches it as if mesmerized. The directors and screenwriters seem to "fear the advent of the television brain, which is supposed to be purely oral and visual, cool, detached, and prone to violence when not engaged in its favorite activity, vegetation."[73] Robert Pattison, in his book *On Literacy,* parodied the harsh stereotype of TV viewers held by the filmmakers and other social critics: "Owners of television minds alternate between states of sexual excitement and narcolepsy. They are routinely manipulated by sinister forces only slightly less mindless than themselves whose object is to strip them of money and dignity while poisoning them with sugar, fluorocarbons, and tawdry dogmas. Anyone exposed to television for protracted periods of time is almost certain to develop narcissism, acne, and fascist tendencies."[74] Pattison dismissed the notion of a TV-drugged culture as unduly alarmist and tinged with nostalgia for a vanished golden age—the more studious, democratic age of print—that never actually existed. But the bleak vision, in film and elsewhere, of a populace tuned in to TV and turned off to experience isn't without its truth.

We live in a wired society that has "substituted images of reality for reality itself."[75] Life is recorded, fragmented, and then replayed in a delirium of colors and sounds. We lurch from calamity to comedy and back again. Dazed and apprehensive, we are vulnerable to the slick come-ons of journalists, advertisers, politicians, therapists—of all those who claim to offer a measure of sympathy and relief. We yearn for comprehension and social contact, and TV, even while it assaults us, provides a sense of community, however fleeting, however false. Longtime newscaster David Brinkley has said, "Watching news is one of the very few things that all of the American people do together. I mean, they sit down together at six or seven P.M. and again at ten or eleven to look at the news.... It has become a kind of national rite...."[76] Yet few are more truly or desperately alone than the average TV viewer, communing with electronic ghosts, touching the hands of shadows, attributing significance to empty figments. Tens of millions pass their nights staring with hungry eyes at the small screen, or restlessly switching channels, seeking something beyond the power of TV to give: absolution and an end to their nameless hurt.

*Medium Cool,* the first film to be directed by Haskell Wexler, the Academy Award-winning cinematographer of *Who's Afraid of Virginia Woolf?*, portrays TV as dehumanizing to both those working behind the cameras and those sitting at home in front of their sets. The title refers to Marshall McLuhan's description of TV as a "cool medium," though the film itself has a decidedly un-McLuhanesque thesis. It argues that TV makes voyeurs of us all by turning carnage into a bizarre form of entertainment. Wexler, who wrote the film and did its photography, told an interviewer: "The first time that millions of Americans actually saw a man being killed was when [Jack] Ruby shot [Lee Harvey] Oswald. They gasped and said, 'I don't believe it.' But then they saw it replayed and replayed and replayed, with the TV announcer saying, 'Now watch Ruby's hand, now watch officer so-and-so's arm as it drops to his side, see Oswald's look of anguish as he doubles up.' The public was watching a scene charged with drama, but one filtered through a glass, a glass protecting them from what people in the past had experienced. When reality comes to you that way, it comes minus one ingredient, and that ingredient is human emotion."[77]

Shot on a lowly $600,000 budget and distributed by Paramount Pictures, *Medium Cool* has a raw immediacy seldom found in the releases of major studios. Abrupt editing, unretouched locations, and a mixed cast of professionals and amateurs all contribute to the film's edgy, authentic atmosphere. Its protagonist, TV cameraman-reporter John Cassellis (Robert Forster), travels through America in the tumultuous spring and summer of 1968, covering Robert Kennedy's funeral, riot training at a National Guard camp, and the street battles outside the Democratic convention in Chicago. By surrounding the fictional narrative with documentary footage, Wexler hoped to capture the strife of the late sixties, and at times he succeeded almost too well. There is an unsettling scene in which the Illinois National Guard lobs tear gas at a group of young demonstrators, and Wexler's sound man is heard to exclaim, "Look out, Haskell, it's real!"

Although *Medium Cool* was only one in a flood of youth-cult films pouring into theaters between 1967 and 1971 (other included *Easy Rider, The Graduate, Alice's Restaurant,* and *Five Easy Pieces*), reviewers praised it as a cinematic breakthrough. The anonymous critic for *Time* asserted, "So strongly does it challenge the usual commercial film techniques and themes that Hollywood, ever wary of both stylistic innovation and contemporary politics, may never recover."[78] Richard Schickel, writing in *Life,* called it "the first entirely serious, commercially sponsored, basically fictional film born of the time of troubles through which this nation has been passing."[79] Vincent Canby of the *New York Times* said, "At its best, 'Medium Cool' is a montage of sheer violence, a warning that our house is on fire and that the roof has already caved in. No other major movie has made that statement so bluntly."[80]

In hailing the film, most reviewers were responding to the gritty documentary sequences, especially of the clashes at the Chicago convention, not to Wexler's fictional narrative. Schickel wrote: "I am not sure Mr. Wexler has entirely solved the esthetic and technical problems that arise when fictional characters are juxtaposed with great events."[81] Canby was less circumspect, saying the characters "are rather lamely worked" into the riots.[82] But whatever its flaws, *Medium Cool* still carries a potent moral: we are as responsible for everything we see as we are for everything we do.[83]

The film opens with John and his sound man Gus (Peter Bonerz) shooting a car accident on a lonely stretch of highway. Instead of helping the injured driver, they unemotionally record the groans, the blood, the twisted metal and shattered glass. They are newsmen first and feeling human beings second. It is only after they get back

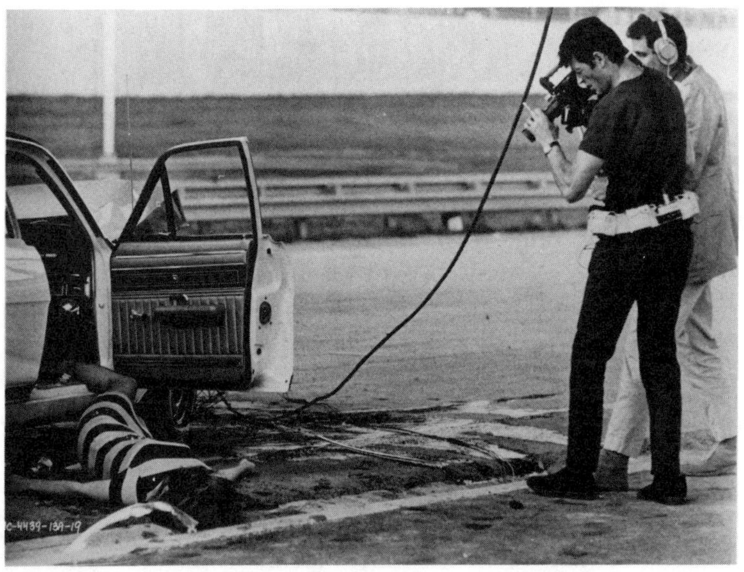

Reporter-cameraman John Cassellis (Robert Forster) and his sound man Gus (Peter Bonerz) are more interested in shooting dramatic news footage than helping an injured driver in *Medium Cool.*

to their company car that John says, almost offhandedly, "Better call an ambulance."

Their callousness is an occupational hazard. Thrust into chaotic situations that threaten to overwhelm them, John and Gus retreat behind the "shopworn shield of journalistic objectivity" or lose themselves in the mechanics of newsgathering.[84] "Jesus, I love to shoot film," John declares, impervious to the tragedy of what he photographs. Gus evades the ethical ambiguities of his job by conceiving of himself as a machine, "a kind of an elongation of a tape recorder," that indiscriminately picks up voices of pain and anger and hate. The stubborn, hypocritical insistence of journalists that their reports neither define nor distort but merely mirror reality is one of the hallmarks of the anti-press film. When the news director of the Chicago station for which John and Gus work says, "We cover the news. We do not manufacture violence," he is reciting an excuse that will be adopted in the 1980s by the slippery editors in *Absence of Malice* and *The Mean Season.*

Wexler tirelessly (skeptics might say tiresomely) contends that TV panders to the bloodthirstiness of the public. "Who wants to see someone sitting, who wants to see someone lying down, who wants to see someone talking peace, unless he's talking loud?" John asks, and the implicit answer is no one. *Medium Cool* is a kaleidoscopic tour of "America the Violent," a land of automobile wrecks, middle-class women at pistol practice, police in riot gear, and black militants spouting fiery rhetoric.[85] At one point, John and his girlfriend attend a roller derby, where the female players brawl and the crowd shouts, "Kill her! Kill her!", "In the crotch! In the crotch!", and other words of encouragement. The scene dissolves to John and the girl making love in his apartment while excited fans continue to chant on the soundtrack, "Go! Go! Go!" A later lovemaking sequence is even more darkly ironic. The camera cuts from the sexual gymnastics to a poster of Edie Adams' famous photograph of a South Vietnamese general blowing away a Viet Cong prisoner. The terrible image serves as a memento mori, a reminder that the violence done in our names or at our instigation comes back to slay us in our beds.

Like the emotionally battered war correspondents of *The Killing Fields, The Year of Living Dangerously, Under Fire,* and *Salvador,* John is ultimately shaken from his professional detachment. First he learns that the station has been allowing the FBI and police to study outtakes. "What am I, a fink?" he screams. "How can I go out and cover a story?" Then he is suddenly and inexplicably fired. In a jerkily photographed, murkily lighted sequence, he runs through long, empty, windowless corridors, desperate to discover the reason for his dismissal. But every door he tries is locked. The corporation that owns the station presents a blank face to the world. It is impossible to pierce the subterfuges of the power structure and pinpoint responsibility. *Medium Cool* shares with the "Hollywood conspiracy films" that came into vogue in the aftermath of the Vietnam War and Watergate—films like *Serpico, Chinatown, The Conversation, The Parallax View,* and *Jaws*—the paranoid belief that government and big business are partners in crime, and that behind paper guarantees of freedom, an invisible hand malignantly rules human affairs.[86]

John's awakening to political consciousness is accompanied by a deepening relationship with a poor widow (Verna Bloom) who has moved to Chicago's ghetto from Appalachia with her 13-year-old son. The romance between the streetwise cameraman and the country innocent is an unlikely bit of plotting, but a likely bit of symbolism. Eileen represents the broken remnants of the old-fashioned rural virtues of modesty, hard work, plain speaking, and kindness. When John takes her in his arms, he figuratively embraces the faded values and ideals of the pre-television age. The film sentimentalizes Eileen, equating her poverty and West Virginia background (which is fleshed out in jarring flashbacks) with natural grace and dignity. But time and the pull of events have foreclosed a return to the garden. The star-spangled dream that the couple will be united in a new, more humane society is introduced mainly so that it can be frustrated. Eileen and her people are orphans of progress. The connection between the past and present has ruptured, and not even love can heal the wound.

On the eve of the Democratic convention, Eileen's son disappears. As she anxiously searches for him into the next day, she passes through a city in chaos and a culture at war with itself. Wexler visually expresses the bitter contradictions of American society by intercutting shots of delegates celebrating inside the convention hall with those of protesters bleeding in the streets. The real-life footage of tanks, troops, night sticks, clouds of tear gas, and cracked skulls calls to mind the apocalyptic vision of history gone wrong in William Butler Yeats' poem, "The Second Coming":

> Things fall apart; the centre cannot hold;
> Mere anarchy is loosed upon the world,
> The blood-dimmed tide is loosed, and everywhere
> The ceremony of innocence is drowned.... [87]

Beneath its self-consciously arty flourishes, the ending of *Medium Cool* is an echo of the beginning. John and Eileen are traveling in a car that spins out of control and slams into a tree, killing her and critically injuring him (the car radio announces the crash before it happens, a surreal touch borrowed from French director Jean-Luc Godard's *Contempt*). Moments later, a working-class brute and his family of grotesques come along the road. Conditioned by TV, they respond to the accident as sheer spectacle, eagerly snapping pictures, and then driving away. The final image—of Wexler on a scaffold pointing what looks like a vintage newsreel camera directly at the audience—demolishes the distance between the voyeurs in the film (newsmen, sports fans, rubbernecks) and the voyeurs in the theater watching the film. While protesters chant on the soundtrack, "The whole world is watching, the whole world is watching," the accusing camera looms larger and larger until we are swallowed by the lens and the screen goes black. It is the black of mourning.

*Network,* a sulphurous satire about the takeover of TV

news by corporate gunslingers and entertainment types, is every bit as bleak as *Medium Cool* in its portrayal of American culture. *Time* called it "the most controversial movie in 1976," which wasn't too much of an exaggeration.[88] The film, directed by Sidney Lumet and written by Paddy Chayefsky, did cause heartburning along Manhattan's "Network Row." Foreshadowing the anger of print journalists at *Absence of Malice,* TV executives blasted the tale of a network ready and able to kill for ratings. "It's a piece of crap," an NBC vice president fumed. "It had nothing to do with our business."[89] But Chayefsky, who made his name (and presumably a fortune) writing for TV in the 1950s, insisted, "Everything in the movie is true—with some extensions."[90]

The film came out at a time when the last traces of the boundary between local news shows and show business were crumbling. Since the early seventies, stations had been hiring consultants to tell them what to cover and how to cover it. The result was fast-paced and entertaining—"a little hit 'em in the guts there, a little soft shoe here, a little sex, a little blood, a taste of something out of the ordinary"—but it was news only in the lowest, loosest sense.[91] In pursuit of bigger ratings, some consultants actually rigged up a cross-section of viewers with electrodes to measure their physical reactions to various newscasters. Anchorman Pat Emory of KNXT-TV in Los Angeles was fired when a test audience failed to tingle properly. "By that measurement," Emory said, "Adolf Hitler should have been an anchorman."[92]

TV consultants weren't the first to discover that stories of stealing and lusting and fighting are guaranteed to sell. From the penny papers of the 1830s through the yellow journals of the 1880s and '90s to the tabloids of the 1920s, the American press grew increasingly proficient at the black art of sensationalism. A poem by Lou Wedema that appeared in the *New York World* of May 27, 1926 more or less describes "gutter journalism" in any age:

Oh, print us views without much news
  Of nudes and sheiks and racing horses,
Knife-battles, mobs, kidnapping clues,

Fire-setting fiends, love theft divorces.
Let's have some warships, railroad wrecks,
A riot caused by racial trouble.
True stories, contests and some sex—
Why, in a week your sales will double.[93]

If sensationalism itself isn't new, the power of TV to penetrate instantly and simultaneously into millions of homes is. It raises the specter of a public brainwashed and benumbed by the rush of images, strung out on cheap thrills. Chayefsky envisioned in *Network* what might happen if ABC, NBC, and CBS, with their huge constituencies and speed-of-light technology, followed the lead of local stations and took a "fun-and-games approach" to the news.[94] And what he foresaw has gradually come to pass. Where once network newscasts defined themselves as electronic newspapers, they now present the day's events as theater. "Everything on television is a show," Don Hewitt, executive producer of the CBS news magazine *60 Minutes,* said in 1985. "The news is a show. *Beverly Hillbillies* is a show. The Super Bowl is a show. The coverage of the assassination of [Egyptian President Anwar] Sadat was a show. That's the nature of the business."[95]

Not all reviewers recognized the prescience of Chayefsky's script. Richard Schickel of *Time* found the plot "so crazily preposterous that even in post-Watergate America—where we know that bats can get loose in the corridors of power—it is just impossible to accept."[96] In any case, the film dominated the 1976 Academy Awards, with Oscars for Peter Finch for best actor, Faye Dunaway for best actress, Beatrice Straight for best supporting actress, and Chayefsky for best original screenplay. It might say something about the complexity of Americans' attitude toward the press that *All the President's Men* received a couple of Oscars that same year. Jason Robards won the best supporting actor award for his portrayal of *Washington Post* editor Ben Bradlee, while William Goldman won for his adaptation of the book by Watergate reporters Bob Woodward and Carl Bernstein.

When *Network* opens, Howard Beale (Finch), veteran anchorman for the UBS network, has just been given two-weeks' notice because of poor ratings. A recent widower and heavy drinker, he is pushed over the edge by his firing and announces on the evening news that he will kill himself on camera in a week. "Should get a hell of a rating," he adds before being dragged off the set. The next day he begs to be allowed on the air one last time to apologize for his outburst. His request is reluctantly granted, but instead of apologizing, he rails against "this demented slaughterhouse of a world we live in" and explains that he has simply run out of the "bullshit" that had kept him going.

Beale's psychotic behavior attracts viewers as his straight delivery of the news never did. Diana Christensen (Dunaway), head of programming, glimpses an opportunity to transform the news—"that dumb show," she calls it—into "the biggest smash on television." It is her theory that "[t]he American people are turning sullen. They have been clobbered on all sides by Vietnam, Watergate, the inflation, the depression. They've turned off, shot up, fucked themselves limp, and nothing helps. So... the American people want somebody to articulate their rage for them." That somebody, she says, is Beale.

Her plan to package Beale as a "latter-day prophet, a magnificent messianic figure inveighing against the hypocrisies of our time," is opposed by network news director Max Schumacher (William Holden). He is an Ed Murrow type, craggy and conscientious, a relic of the era when anchormen were journalists, not actors. "[Beale] needs care and treatment," he protests, "and all you grave robbers care about is that he's a hit." Shumacher loses the argument—and his job. Frank Hackett (rhymes with hatchet; Robert Duvall), chief of operations for CCA, the corporation that owns the network and that, in turn, is owned by the Arabs—it gets complicated, rather like this sentence—hands the news division over to Diana.

Before you can say "A.C. Nielsen," she has sexed up the news by adding a studio audience and carnival acts:

"Sybil the Soothsayer," "Mata Hari and Her Skeletons in the Closet," and, of course, "The Mad Prophet of the Airwaves, Howard Beale." The program immediately jumps to near the top of the ratings. Diana also scores with "The Mao Tse-tung Hour," a series in which the Ecumenical Liberation Army robs, kidnaps, kills, and commits other authentic acts of terrorism. UBS literally gets away with murder "by standing," as Diana laughingly explains, "on the First Amendment, freedom of the press, and the right to protect our sources." (In *The Almighty,* a 1982 schlock-buster by Irving Wallace, a media baron similarly hires a terrorist gang to create exclusive news for his papers and TV stations. There seems to be a feeling abroad that journalists are no better than terrorists, using VDTs and videotape to sow violence and chaos and hysterical fear.)

Hollywood films are the products of Corporationland, designed with careful attention to the latest box-office trends. Paradoxically, this didn't deter the makers of *Network* from alleging that TV is too powerful and pervasive to be entrusted to good little corporate soldiers who blindly obey the commands of the marketplace. "When the 12th largest company in the world, the Communications Corporation of America, controls the most awesome goddamn force in the whole godless world, who knows what shit will be peddled as truth?" Beale says. The poor bastard may be certifiably insane, hearing voices and wandering the city at night in his pajamas, but his harangues against TV are still somehow lucid and affecting. He cautions his viewers:

> Television is not the truth. Television is a goddamn amusement park. Television is a circus, a carnival.... We're in the boredom-killing business. So if you want the truth, go to God, go to your guru, go to yourself, because that's the only place you're ever going to find any real truth.... Man, you'll never get any truth from us.... We'll tell you any shit you want to hear. We deal in illusions, man, none of it is true. But you people sit there night after night, day after day, all ages, colors, creeds. We're all you know. You're beginning to believe the

Anchorman Howard Beale (Peter Finch) goes raving mad in *Network*—to the delight of TV viewers and the profitability of the Communications Corporation of America.

> illusions we're spinning here. You're beginning to think that the tube is reality, and your own lives are unreal. You do whatever the tube tells you. You dress like the tube, eat like the tube, raise your children like the tube.... This is mass madness, you maniacs.

*Network* exploits the old romantic conceit that the apparently crazy are really sane, and that the apparently sane are really crazy. Beale invites the public to join in his exalted madness, to become converts to his lunacy. "First you got to get mad," he advises the millions watching at home. "You got to say I'm a human being, goddammit. My life has value." He tells them to open their windows, stick their heads out, and scream, "I'm mad as hell, and I'm not going to take it anymore," and all over the country, people do exactly as he asks. The readiness of the audience to pick up and repeat the slogan can be variously interpreted. But to me it suggests not so much the shattering of "mind-forg'd manacles" as their eerie clanking, not so much cleansing anger as creeping zombiism.[97]

Beale is a boozy, baggy-pants version of Schumacher, the Puritan conscience of the film. Both are mouthpieces for Chayefsky's attacks on TV and victims of Diana's ruthlessness. There is a soap-opera subplot in which Schumacher leaves his kind, noble, understanding wife (Straight) and has a May-December affair with Diana. But Diana is TV generation, she "learned life from Bugs Bunny," and is incapable of any real feeling. In bed, on top of Schumacher, she talks ratings until orgasm. The film holds the sexually emancipated, professionally ambitious woman of the seventies in horror. She is a beautiful and deadly lie, a devourer, a black widow. Schumacher calls Diana "television incarnate"—meaning that she is symptomatic of what is wrong with contemporary society. "War, murder, death are all the same to you as bottles of beer," he says, "and the daily business of life is a corrupt comedy.... You're madness, Diana, virulent madness. Everything you touch dies with you." He goes back to his wife and home, the circle of safety, and considers his retreat a victory over darkness and ruin.

But there is no going back for Beale. Mr. Jensen (Ned Beatty), the porcine president of CCA, grows alarmed about Beale's anti-establishment message and summons him to a private meeting. "You get up on your little 21-inch screen and howl about America and democracy," Jensen says in a booming voice that the frayed, confused Beale mistakes for God's. "There is no America, there is no democracy. There is only IBM and ITT and AT&T and DuPont, Dow, Union Carbide, and Exxon. Those are the nations of the world today. . . . " Entranced by Jensen, the mad prophet begins to preach that dehumanization isn't such a bad word, but no one wants to hear that the "individual is finished," even if—or especially if—it is true. His ratings plummet, threatening the profitability of the entire network. "So what are we going to do about this Beale son of a bitch?" a worried UBS executive asks. Diana proposes that the Ecumenical Liberation Army assassinate him on the air (it will be a "helluva kickoff show" for the new season), and Beale becomes "the first known instance of a man who was killed because he had lousy ratings."

The savage portrayal of TV in *Network* and other movies may stem in part from simple envy. In 1951 weekly movie attendance in the United States was 90 million, but slid by the end of the decade to 43 million.[98] TV has displaced moviegoing as the most popular form of entertainment, and moviemakers seem never to have forgotten nor forgiven that. *Network,* in effect, harries TV for usurping the prerogative of movies to provide escape—for turning escapism into a daily custom. And when the public tends to tire quickly of serious issues and demand theater, the journalist, as Russell Baker of the *New York Times* remarked, is "like the guy who used to stand outside tents working his mouth to draw a crowd."[99]

Such is the role of Patrick Hale (Sean Connery), the globe-trotting TV correspondent in *Wrong Is Right* (1982), which was written, directed, and produced by former journalist Richard Brooks and based on the novel *The Better Angels* by Charles McCarry. The sardonic Hale acts as a sort of master of ceremonies at Armageddon, presenting loony skits of death and destruction between commer-

Superstar TV correspondent Patrick Hale (Sean Connery) brings his patented smirk to coverage of a demonstration in *Wrong Is Right.*

cials. "Make 'em laugh, make 'em cry, make 'em buy and buy and buy," he self-mockingly chants. There is little new in this, and the critical reaction to the film was in some ways more revealing than the film itself. Reviewers described it (admiringly in the case of Judith Crist) as an attempt to update Stanley Kubrick's black comic masterpiece, *Dr. Strangelove* (1964).[100] The comparison was impossibly overblown, but did illustrate that in the six years since *Network*—six long years of "happy talk" news shows, celebrity journalists, and spiraling sensationalism—black comedy had become the accepted mode for depicting how thoroughly TV has brutalized human nature.

The plot of *Wrong Is Right* concerns the pandemonium and political intrigue that erupt when two homemade atom bombs go up for sale on the open market. Among the large cast of characters (actually, caricatures) are brainwashed terrorists, oil-rich sheiks, a Texas demagogue, and supersecret spies. The humor is pretty feeble—unless you find hilarious lines like "He's crazy enough to be insane." But if the film lacks Chayefsky's astringent wit and Lumet's manic direction, it fully shares *Network*'s contempt for TV.

Hale's boss (Robert Webber) is obsessed with ratings and revenues. After the broadcast of an investigative story, he worries aloud, "It could be slander, it could be libel. Even worse, it could be a drop in the Nielsen ratings." The film portrays ours as a time of twisted loyalties and inverted values, when light is dark, foul is fair, and TV is reality. "Remember," one member of a terrorist suicide squad tells another, "you've got to be seen. If it doesn't happen on television, it means nothing." The world is a stage, and kings, presidents, war-mad generals, and assassins strut their stuff for the cameras in swift, mind-numbing succession. "We peddle disaster . . . ," Hale says. "Blood and tears, football and cheers, performers, superstars. Get 'em on, get 'em off, next, next, fast, fast. We're in the entertainment business."

There is a tremendous gulf between *Wrong Is Right* and Brooks' 1951 film, *Deadline U.S.A.*, starring Humphrey Bogart as the managing editor of a dying metropolitan daily. The earlier film, despite plenty of signs that all isn't well with the press (the *Day* is about to be sold by its absentee owners to a competitor and phased out), still shows journalists working for the public good. Rather than quietly fading away, the paper exposes an underworld czar in a final glorious burst of crusading. "It may not be the oldest profession," Bogart idealistically says of journalism, "but it's the best." Idealism degenerates into opportunism, and the best into the worst, in *Wrong Is Right.* In the decades since *Deadline U.S.A.*, society had grown so contaminated and chaotic that the notion of looking to the press, or any institution, for answers was now laughable. TV journalists were hucksters, perverts, or jerks, and it required a blind effort of will to pull a happy ending from out of the void.

*Power*—directed by Lumet and written by David Himmelstein, once a press aide to former Massachusetts Sen. Edward Brooke—offers not one ending, but two, the first soothing, the second forbidding. Taken together, they demonstrate the difficulty of keeping faith with a vision of moral rebirth in an age in which image has overwhelmed reality and nothing is what it seems.

The film follows hotshot media consultant Pete St. John (Richard Gere) as he applies his magic to anyone able to afford his $25,000-a-month retainer, from a Central American despot to an Ohio industrialist running for the Senate with the sinister support of Arab oil interests. St. John is a Faustian figure, bartering away his soul for a godlike power over political life and death. Zooming between campaign stops in his private jet, he plugs in his Walkman and raps out paradiddles on a rubber pad to muffle the cries of his conscience. His ultramodern office in New York epitomizes his isolation and corruption. It is cool, dim, vaultlike, full of oblique lines and seductive shadows. When he discovers that the office has been bugged by agents of the Arabs, it is as if his professional identity has risen up against him. The film calculates the price of substituting money for moral values, computer printouts for commitment, image for real feeling. In the final accounting, the price is self-betrayal.

For all the similarity in theme between *Power* and *Network,* the films express the theme differently. The nihilistic humor of *Network* is abandoned in *Power* for a more cautious style of attack, one that doesn't absolutely rule out the possibility of redemption. And the main target of attack shifts from the electronic news media to media consultants, gray eminences who contemptuously manipulate the press just as the press contemptuously manipulates the public. "Every time we hit a new media market," St. John explains to a client, "we'll have remotes set up for the noon and six o'clock. The local anchors don't know shit, even less than the reporters. This way we'll be able to get our message straight through, no interruptions."

The one wide-awake reporter in the film, St. John's former wife Ellen Freeman (Julie Christie), Washington correspondent for a London newspaper, might as well be napping. Her keen nose for scandal is set twitching by the surprise announcement that Sam Hastings (E.G. Marshall), a liberal stalwart of the Senate, won't seek reelection. He cites ill health, but is actually being blackmailed by the oil lobby. As Ellen digs for the truth, the film can't quite decide whether to congratulate or condemn her. One moment a panicky conspirator is saying, "She's a problem, no matter how you cut it"; the next, St. John is yelling in her face: "You're praying so hard [Hastings is] fucked up, you're salivating.... You're fucked up, not him." From the screenplay's muddled perspective, her confrontation with St. John has a tonic effect, for she later suppresses her hunger for a scoop and drops the story out of sympathy for Hastings and his family. What is missing is a little sympathy for her misled readers.

St. John himself undergoes a sudden change of heart at the end of the picture. "Maybe it takes too much in America—too much energy, too much attention—to follow it all," he tells a young college professor (Matt Salinger) who is quixotically running for Hastings' seat. "Maybe they like to get the candidates prepackaged, predigested, like TV dinners. I've become a very rich man believing that. Prove me wrong." The professor does—sort of—by campaigning on the issues and unexpectedly finishing second, instead of third, in the race. But the film can't sustain the illusion that an also-ran is the same as a winner, nor does it really try to. "We've come too far to turn back now," Salinger declares in his "victory" speech, hopeful words that are given an ominous twist when the film segues into its closing sequence—a long, slow pan of computers and TV equipment whirring and flashing while "The Stars and Stripes Forever" booms on the soundtrack like a mad dirge for American democracy.

If film is a "cultural metaphor," a mirror of the collective mind, then journalists are right to be alarmed by movies like *Power, Network, The Mean Season,* and *Absence of Malice,* which portray them as monsters of hypocrisy and greed.[101] Public distrust of the press is real and deeply rooted, not simply something dreamed up by a bunch of screenwriters. But anti-press films reflect and reinforce, feed on and feed, the distrust. From the late 1960s through the mid-1980s, Hollywood has treated audiences to a parade of reckless reporters, cynical editors, and money-crazed corporate executives who crush reputations and lives for a scoop or ratings point. The films about the fractured world of TV are especially bitter, suggesting that as technology has advanced, morality has declined, and that terror and death ride the airwaves. *Wrong Is Right* draws an explicit parallel between communication satellites on the one hand and the Bomb on the other. The information explosion and the nuclear fireball are, as it were, technological cousins, each with its own form of fatal, and inescapable, fallout. In anti-press films, journalists are made the scapegoats for the tragic predicament of modern man, imprisoned by his fantasies and mocked by his machines.

## Notes

1. After tryouts in Atlantic City, *The Front Page* opened on August 14, 1928, at the Times Square Theater in New York, where it ran an impressive 276 performances. The book version of the script was published the same month the play opened and sold through six printings in the first year.

The first film version was directed by Lewis Milestone and written by Bartlett Cormack, with additional dialogue by Charles Lederer and Hecht. Adolphe Menjou played editor Walter Burns, and Pat O'Brien was star reporter Hildy Johnson.

The second film version, retitled *His Girl Friday,* was directed by Howard Hawks and written by Lederer. Hildy, as the new title indicates, was now a woman (Rosalind Russell), the ex-wife of Burns (Cary Grant). To the war of nerves between editor and reporter was thus added the battle of the sexes. The result was a classic—perhaps *the* classic—screwball comedy.

In 1949 there was a short-lived TV series based on the play.

The 1974 version was directed by former reporter Billy Wilder, who wrote the screenplay with I.A.L. Diamond. Walter Matthau made an inspired Burns, playing the role with a noisy vulgarity that seemed more appropriate to the character than the suaveness of either Menjou or Grant, but Jack Lemmon was woefully miscast as Hildy.

The latest, though probably not the last, version was *Switching Channels,* set in a TV newsroom. Released in March 1988, the film was directed by Ted Kotcheff, and starred Kathleen Turner and Burt Reynolds. Critics disliked it. "Does the world really need yet another film version of 'The Front Page'?" Jack Garner of Gannett News Service asked, and answered: "If it's going to be 'Switching Channels,' I think not." *Poughkeepsie Journal,* 4 March 1988, p. 2D.

For an excellent overview of the long and varied history of *The Front Page,* see Doug Fetherling, *The Five Lives of Ben Hecht* (Canada.: Lester and Orpen, 1977), particularly pp. 67–86.

2. Carlos Clarens, *Crime Movies: From Griffith to The Godfather and Beyond* (New York: W.W. Norton, 1981), p. 104.

3. Nora Sayre, "Falling Prey to Parodies of the Press," January 1, 1975, *New York Times Encyclopedia of Film* (New York: Times Books, 1984), unpaged.

4. Desmond Ryan, "The Hollywood Reporter," *Washington Journalism Review,* September 1985, p. 46.

5. Norman Isaacs, *Untended Gates: The Mismanaged Press* (New York: Columbia University Press, 1986), p. 99.

6. David Shaw, "On Arrogance and Accountability in the Press," address sponsored by the Carol Burnett Fund for Responsible Journalism, University of Hawaii, 8 March 1983.

7. Isaacs, *Untended Gates,* p. 154.

8. James W. Carey, "A Plea for the University Tradition," presidential address to the Association for Education in Journalism, Seattle, Wash., 13 August 1978.

9. Quoted in H. Eugene Goodwin, *Groping for Ethics in Journalism* (Ames: Iowa State University Press, 1983), p. 257.

10. J. Edward Murray, "Quality News Versus Junk News," *Neiman Reports,* Summer 1984, p. 14.

11. Williams A. Henry, III, "Journalism Under Fire," *Time,* December 12, 1983, p. 76.

12. Katherine Winton Evans, "National Security and the Press," *Washington Journalism Review,* July 1986, p. 14.

13. "Letters," *Time,* June 9, 1986, p. 9.

14. "Mirror, mirror on the wall . . . ," *Columbia Journalism Review,* March/April 1986, p. 24.

15. *The People & The Press: A Times Mirror Investigation of Public Attitudes Toward the News Media, Conducted by The Gallup*

*Organization* (Los Angeles: Times Mirror, 1986), p. 16.

16. *Ibid.,* pp. 20–21.
17. *Ibid.,* p. 4.
18. *Ibid.,* p. 30.
19. *Ibid.,* pp. 30–31.
20. Isaacs, *Untended Gates,* pp. 21–22.
21. Robert Sherrill, "News Ethics: Press & Jerks," *Grand Street,* Winter 1986, p. 127.
22. Murray, "Quality News," p. 15.
23. Neil Postman, *Amusing Ourselves to Death* (New York: Viking, 1985), p. 106.
24. Quoted in Isaacs, *Untended Gates,* p. 44.
25. "A Conversation With Neil Postman: TV 'Has Culture by the Throat,' " *U.S. News & World Reports,* December 23, 1985, p. 58.
26. Gerald Weales, *Canned Goods as Caviar: American Film Comedy of the 1930s* (Chicago: University of Chicago Press, 1985), p. 2.
27. Geraldine Fabrikant, "Ted Turner's Screen Test," *New York Times,* 30 March 1986, sec. 3, p. 1.
28. *Ibid.,* p. 8.
29. Karen Rothmeyer, "Hot properties: the media-buying spree explained," *Columbia Journalism Review,* November/December 1985, p. 38.
30. Murray, "Quality News," p. 16.
31. Rothmeyer, "Hot properties," p. 43.
32. Quoted in *ibid.,* p. 39.
33. Robert Hatch, "Absence of Malice," *Nation,* January 29, 1982, p. 27.
34. Lucinda Franks, "Hollywood Update," *Columbia Journalism Review,* November/December 1981, p. 63.
35. Ryan, "Hollywood Reporter," p. 37.
36. Hatch, "Absence of Malice," p. 27.
37. Quoted in Clifford Christians, Kim B. Rotzoll, and Mark Fackler, *Media Ethics: Cases and Moral Reasoning* (New York: Longman, 1983), p. 80.
38. Hatch, "Absence of Malice," p. 27.
39. Jonathan Friendly, "A Movie On the Press Stirs a Debate," *New York Times,* 15 November 1981, sec. 2, p. 1.
40. Richard Schickel, "Lethal Leaks," *Time,* November 23, 1981, p. 98.
41. Franks, "Hollywood Update," p. 59.
42. *Ibid.,* p. 63.

43. Quoted in Friendly, "Movie Stirs Debate," p. 26.
44. Ryan, "Hollywood Reporter," p. 47.
45. *Ibid.;* Franks, "Hollywood Update," p. 63.
46. Isaacs, *Untended Gates,* pp. 77–78.
47. Franks, "Hollywood Update," p. 63.
48. Isaacs, *Untended Gates,* p. 163.
49. Christians, *Media Ethics,* p. 154.
50. Quoted in Jane Gross, "An Actor Explores The Fourth Estate," *New York Times,* 10 February 1985, sec 2, p. 19.
51. Quoted in *ibid.*
52. *Ibid.,* pp. 1, 19.
53. Vincent Canby, "A Journalism Movie That Raises Tough Questions," *New York Times,* 3 March 1985, sec. 2, p. 17.
54. Quoted in Goodwin, *Groping for Ethics,* p. 164.
55. John M. Phelan, *Disenchantment: Meaning and Morality in the Media* (New York: Hastings House, 1980), p. 20.
56. Postman, *Amusing Ourselves,* p. 87.
57. Edwin Diamond, *The Tin Kazoo: Television, Politics, and the News* (Cambridge, Mass.: MIT Press, 1975), p. 13.
58. See John J. O'Connor, "The 'Vast Wasteland,' 25 Years Later," *New York Times,* 4 May 1986, sec. 2, pp. 1, 29.
59. Diamond, *Tin Kazoo,* p. 61.
60. Alex S. Jones, "The Anchors," *New York Times Magazine,* 27 July 1986, p. 13.
61. Diamond, *Tin Kazoo,* pp. 92–93.
62. Bob Teague, *Live and Off Color: News Biz* (New York: A & W Publishers, 1982), pp. 16–17.
63. Jones, "Anchors," p. 16.
64. Quoted in Teague, *Live and Off Color,* p. 43.
65. Henry David Thoreau, *Walden and Other Writings of Henry David Thoreau* (New York: Modern Library, 1937), p. 47.
66. Burton Benjamin, "TV Network News Finds The Rules Have Changed," *New York Times,* 17 August 1986, sec. 2, p. 25.
67. Teague, *Live and Off Color,* pp. 116–17.
68. Diamond, *Tin Kazoo,* p. 83.
69. Mark R. Levy and John P. Robinson, "The 'huh?' factor: untangling TV news," *Columbia Journalism Review,* July/August 1986, pp. 48–49.
70. Quoted in Isaacs, *Untended Gates,* p. 219.
71. Christopher Lasch. *The Culture of Narcissism: American Life in an Age of Diminishing Expectations* (New York: Warner Books, 1979), p. 130.

72. Postman, *Amusing Ourselves,* p. 105.

73. Robert Pattison, *On Literacy: The Politics of the Word from Homer to the Age of Rock* (Oxford: Oxford University Press, 1982), p. 114.

74. *Ibid.*

75. Lasch, *Culture of Narcissism,* p. 375.

76. Quoted in Teague, *Live and Off Color,* p. 218.

77. Quoted in Guy Flatley, "Chicago and Other Violences," *New York Times,* 7 September 1969, sec. 2, p. 19.

78. "Dynamite," *Times,* August 22, 1969, p. 62.

79. Richard Schickel, "A Film for Us Voyeurs of Violence," *Life,* August 15, 1969, p. 14.

80. Vincent Canby, "Our Time: Arlo and Chicago," *New York Times,* 31 August 1969, sec. 2, p. 35.

81. Schickel, "Voyeurs of Violence," p. 14.

82. Canby, "Our Time," p. 35.

83. I am paraphrasing Michael Herr, who drew this moral from his harrowing experiences as a war correspondent in Vietnam. *Dispatches* (New York: Avon Books, 1978), p. 207.

84. "Dynamite," *Time,* p. 62.

85. Flatley, "Chicago and Other Violences," p. 19.

86. The phrase belongs to Cagin and Dray, who identify and analyze these films as a distinct genre in *Hollywood Films of the Seventies,* pp. 203–11.

87. William Butler Yeats, "The Second Coming," in *Selected Poems and Two Plays of William Butler Yeats* (New York: Macmillan, 1962), p. 91.

88. "The Movie TV Loves to Hate", *Time,* December 13, 1976, p. 78.

89. Quoted in *ibid.*

90. Quoted in *ibid.,* p. 79.

91. Teague, *Live and Off Color,* p. 99.

92. Quoted in "Movie TV Loves to Hate," p. 79.

93. Quoted in Simon Michael Bessie, *Jazz Journalism* (New York: Dutton, 1938; reprint ed., New York: Russel & Russel, 1969), p. 18.

94. Teague, *Live and Off Color,* p. 31.

95. Donald Fry, ed., *Believing the News* (St. Petersburg, Fla.: Poynter Institute for Media Studies, 1985), p. 62.

96. Richard Schickel, "The Upper Depths," *Time,* November 29, 1976, p. 79.

97. The phrase is from William Blake's "London," *Blake,* Laurel Poetry Series (New York: Dell, 1960), p. 64.

98. Michael Wood, *America in the Movies* (New York: Basic Books, 1975), p. 12.

99. Russell Baker, "A Time for Barkers," in *Believing the News,* p. 260.

100. Judith Crist, "A 'Dr. Strangelove' for the 1980s," *Saturday Review,* May 1982, p. 54.

101. Jack Shadion, *Dreams and Dead Ends: The American Gangster/Crime Film* (Cambridge, Mass.: MIT Press, 1979), p. x.

# THE WALLS CAME TUMBLING DOWN

> Is there any institution that isn't corrupt to its very foundations? Don't you believe it.—Finley Peter Dunne's "Mr. Dooley"

IN THE FALL OF 1973, while the Watergate drama was still unfolding in courtrooms and congressional committee rooms and on front pages, *New York* magazine declared the investigative reporter the "new American folk hero." The chronicle of pop culture asserted in its hyperthyroid prose that "[a]rmed only with his conscience and his wits," the investigative reporter "makes whole governments tremble, not to mention mere politicians and other millionaires.... He is the glamour boy of journalism—in a country suddenly without glamour anywhere. To a nation unsure of its leaders and itself, he seems to offer certitude."[1]

It was a claim others would echo, sometimes with eagerness and pride, sometimes with irony and resignation, down the rest of the decade. "Foreign assignments," Lou Cannon of the *Washington Post* commented in 1977, "were once the glamour beats of journalism.... The bloom has faded from that particular rose, and the 'investigative reporter' has replaced the foreign correspondent as the current vogue of journalism."[2] The following year, *New York Times* columnist Tom Wicker wrote that the investigative reporter had taken over "the role played at various times in the American psyche by so many robust earlier heroes—Paul Revere, the watchman of liberty; the Western sheriff...singlehandedly guaranteeing law and order; Lindbergh challenging the Atlantic in the name of progress—the fearless, fighting individual standing up for the many, daring the gods, alert on the barricades."[3]

Such remarks almost make it sound as if investigative reporting were an invention of the 1970s, which was anything but the case. From roughly 1902 to 1912, journalist reformers—dubbed "muckrakers" by President Theodore Roosevelt in a fit of pique over their audacity—tried to rouse the middle class with exposés of corruption in government and business. Writing for new national magazines like *McClure's, Everybody's, Collier's* and William Randolph Hearst's *Cosmopolitan,* they revealed, as the titles of their articles said, "The Shame of the Cities," "The Treason of the Senate," "Frenzied Finance," and "The Great American Fraud."[4]

Before the turn of the century, the crusading spirit was crackling in the sensational, or "yellow," journals. In 1883 Joseph Pulitzer promised in his first edition of the *New York World* that the paper would "expose all fraud and sham, fight all public evils and abuses [and] serve and battle for the people with earnest sincerity."[5] And he more or less kept his word as he sought to identify the *World* with the interests of its lowbrow audience of immigrants, factory workers, and shopgirls. It was, however, the penny papers of the 1830s that made perhaps the most romantic contribution to the investigative tradition of journalism, the detective reporter. He would chase criminals, exasperate police, score scoops, and entertain readers well into the 1920s. As novelist (and when debts piled up, Hearst reporter) Jack London once advised a cub, the public "has a keen appetite for sensational and scandalous news. Newspapers offer the greatest prizes to unravelers of crime."[6]

Although investigative reporting has a long and venerable history, it is sheer illusion that muckraking is rampant in the press. "Traditionally," Paul H. Weaver pointed out, "American journalism has been very close to, dependent upon, and cooperative with, official sources."[7] A reporter who challenges the official version of events risks a lot: "lost access, complaints to editors and publishers, social penalties, leaks to competitors.... "[8] This only makes the eruption of investigative reporting from the late 1960s to the mid-1970s seem all the more remarkable. What underlay the outburst was the press' realization that it had been badly used by the government in recent years. Instances included its thoughtless acquiescence in Senator Joseph McCarthy's red-hunting; the Eisenhower administration's lies about the U-2 flights over the Soviet Union; and President Kennedy's request to the *New York Times* to soft-pedal a story on the impending invasion of the Bay of Pigs in Cuba and his later criticism of the *Times* for doing as he had asked.[9] The final shock to the old cozy press-government relationship was Vietnam, especially after the leak of the Pentagon Papers in 1971 disclosed massive duplicity in the conduct of the war. I.F. Stone spoke for a growing number of journalists when he said, "Every government is run by liars and thieves, and nothing they say should be believed."[10]

A newly truculent press rushed out to find wrongdoing and found plenty of it. Seymour Hersh exposed the My Lai massacre and the secret bombing of Cambodia. Stanley Penn of the *Wall Street Journal* uncovered corporate bribery of foreign officials. William Lambert of *Life* magazine drove U.S. Supreme Court Justice Abe Fortas from the bench with a story about Fortas' $20,000 retainer from the private foundation of an indicted financier.[11] The *Cleveland Plain-Dealer,* the *Chicago Tribune,* the *Boston Globe, Newsday,* and even the old-line Associated Press assembled teams of investigative reporters.[12] CBS launched the news magazine *60 Minutes,* featuring correspondent Mike Wallace as a sort of beetle-browed, gravelly voiced personification of journalistic aggressiveness.

Looking back, one can clearly see that the wave of investigative journalism crested with Watergate and the resignation of President Nixon. "Never before," Michael Schudson wrote, "had there been a national symbol of enterprise reporting of even remotely comparable substance and scope—and effect."[13] David Laventhol, publisher of *Newsday,* called Watergate "the finest moment in print journalism, maybe in the whole country."[14] Bob

Woodward and Carl Bernstein of the *Washington Post,* who almost had an exclusive patent on Watergate stories in the early phase of the scandal, became special heroes. Journalism schools filled to overflowing with young people aspiring to be the next Woodward or Bernstein.[15] The investigative tide swept as swiftly through city rooms as through college classrooms. In 1974 four of the six Pulitzer Prizes for newspaper writing were awarded for investigative reporting.[16]

Ironically, the spread of muckraking spelled its demise. Like the original muckrakers, the new generation came to seem guilty of overkill. The public resented reading and hearing all that bad news. As a backlash set in, the press did a regrettable, if predictable, thing—it began to devour its own children. "Investigative reporting now colors everything we try to do," Haynes Johnson of the *Post* complained to colleague Lou Cannon. "Many of the stories which are pursued today have been exposed over and over in the past decade. What is the purpose of it…? Much of it is mindlessness that has no meaning."[17] Others expanded on his criticism as the seventies slipped into the conservative eighties and the press' rating in opinion polls continued to dive. In 1983 Frank McCulloch, executive editor of McClatchy Newspapers, told a conference of investigative reporters: "We have become too full of ourselves. We have been arrogant. We have been rude. We have been elitist. We have been inaccurate. We have been insensitive. We have been unfair…."[18] At the same meeting, J.D. Alexander, managing editor of the *San Diego Union,* assailed reporters who are "without compassion and see evil at every turn."[19]

Journalists now try to win public forgiveness by freely confessing to having had after Watergate a wild craving for blood that could only be satisfied by a constant supply of fresh victims. Not long ago, veteran TV journalist Barbara Matusow said: "The press almost too gleefully jumped into its role as the opposition, and this role offends many people…for the press…to see itself as the only check on government and to operate on that assumption is very poor service to the public."[20] The investigative reporter has been pulled off his pedestal, and the pedestal left to molder. Consider in proof that "Irangate," which tarnished President Reagan's last term, was brought to light not by Washington correspondents, but by an obscure magazine in Lebanon.

If the investigative reporter has been treated at times as a liability by the rest of the press, he has proved an endless boon to fictioneers and filmmakers—a figure of recurring topical interest who also can be shaped to reflect traditional ideas and values. Novels about crusading journalists, such as Joseph A. Altsheler's *Gutherie of the Times* (1904) and Jesse Lynch Williams' *The Day-Dreamer* (1906), formed a background accompaniment to the muckraking of the Progressive Era. By the mid-1930s, the detective reporter was a familiar presence on the screen, cracking jokes and murder cases at the expense of dim-witted police, and for the next twenty years his irreverent style of crime detection would be celebrated in a string of all but identical B pictures. Even their titles were barely distinguishable from each other: *Behind the Evidence* (1935), *Behind the Headlines* (1937), and *Behind the News* (1941); *Man Hunt* (1936) and *Midnight Manhunt* (1945); *While New York Sleeps* (1938) and *While the City Sleeps* (1955).

The investigative reporters in more recent films may have a hard, glossy overcoating of professionalism, but beneath it the heart of the old detective reporter still beats briskly. They are portrayed as a rare breed, rugged individualists in an increasingly bureaucratic profession. Over the opposition of corrupt or cautious editors, they probe a sensitive issue like nuclear power and learn that supposedly legitimate institutions are hives of vast, sinister conspiracies. The shooting of President Kennedy in Dallas on November 22, 1963 had helped plant suspicions that invisible conspirators were stage-managing history. Five years later, conspiracy theories were so numerous—there were at least twenty-one by one count—that *Esquire* published "A Primer of Assassination Theories."[21] The Hollywood dream factory processed the belief in cabals, and the longing for clearly labeled causes and effects, according to its own special formula.[22] The *films noir* of the 1940s, which were steeped in shadows and postwar anxieties, had originated the visual vocabulary for conjuring up an atmosphere of doubt and dread: dark, rain-slick streets, lurid flashes of neon, anonymous office buildings, and empty, mazelike corridors. Investigative reporters enter a nightmare world where the boundaries of reality keep shifting, a paranoid world where men of high repute secretly plot robbery and murder.[23]

There is diversity within this narrative framework. Depending on the film, the investigative reporter may be a victim, comedian, penitent, or knight-errant. It all adds up to a convoluted and, in some ways, tragic portrait. The reporter's search into hidden crimes is related to myths in which discovering the name of a monster or guessing its riddle breaks a terrible thralldom.[24] One such myth concerns the Sphinx, a creature with the head and breast of a woman, the body of a lion, and the wings of an eagle. Perched on a cliff outside of Thebes, she posed a riddle to travelers, killing them when they answered incorrectly. Oedipus heard of the city's plight, climbed the cliff, and solved the riddle. Enraged, the Sphinx threw herself to her death. But the story of Oedipus, as we all know, doesn't end there. It ends in patricide, incest, blindness, and eternal wandering.

## *The Investigative Reporter As Victim:* Black Like Me *(1964),* The Parallax View *(1974), and* Fever Pitch *(1985)*

> Now you go into oblivion.—Doctor to John Howard Griffin, author of *Black Like Me*

What characterized American films from the thirties through the fifties, John Simon has written, was the happy ending. So much so that a neologism appeared in several

European languages, "happyend." It meant "a joyous resolution of complicated intrigues and overwhelming problems, allowing the hero and heroine to fall in the last shot, against all probability, into each other's arms and live, by implication, happy ever after."[25]

The feeling of a "cellophane-wrapped 'Ever After' " in Hollywood films suggested that America was the land of the optimistic and the home of the naive.[26] All that would change, and change drastically, in the sixties and seventies. The country was convulsed by race riots, Vietnam, political assassinations, Watergate—by apocalyptic fevers and sudden mysterious chills. Americans weren't so innocent or confident anymore.

As a popular rather than an elite art form, movies can't afford to lose touch with the attitudes of moviegoers. The new sense of vulnerability was soon reflected in disaster films like *The Poseidon Adventure, Airport '75, Earthquake,* and *The Towering Inferno;* in vigilante films like *Death Wish, Billy Jack,* and *Walking Tall;* and in paranoid thrillers like *Klute* and *Three Days of the Condor.* Some of the films that featured an investigative reporter combined the bleakest elements of all the other genres.

*Black Like Me* was the first directorial effort of Long Island film editor Carl Lerner, who wrote the screenplay with his wife. The film was based on John Howard Griffin's best seller, which had been serialized in *Sepia,* a national black magazine. Written before the era of freedom rides and sit-ins, the book purports to tell "what is like to be a Negro in a land where we keep the Negro down."[27] In 1959 Griffin darkened his skin with medication, sun-lamp treatments, and stain, and traveled through the Deep South as a black. His diary of his seven weeks in limbo created a sensation when it was published. Not only was he in demand for TV interviews, but racists burned his effigy on the main street of his hometown of Mansfield, Texas.

To avoid interference from extremist groups, the film was shot in Maryland, Virginia, Florida, and Washington under the working title of *No Man Walks Alone.*[28] It was released in 1964, the same year a major civil rights bill was passed. Lerner claimed: "Our sole function as artists was to make a motion picture in which we believed. We wanted it to be authentic.... "[29] But reviewers found the film hackneyed, as well as technically inept. "What may have started out as a seriously conceived cinematic version of Griffin's book," *Variety* said, "wound up as a wishy-washy effort that will do the cause of integration little good." *Newsweek* called the film "dreary" and "pointless." Particularly annoying to reviewers was James Whitmore's obvious make-up. *Variety* gibed that Whitmore, as journalist John Finley Horton, "looks like a high-school Othello," and *Newsweek*, that "he hardly looks human."[30]

Before Horton can begin his strange odyssey, he must overcome the objections of the publisher of *Black and Tan* magazine. "It's a scoop," admits the white Texas millionaire, "but it's much too dangerous. You got to forget it." Horton can't. On earlier assignments, he was "neutral, a reporter." "This," he declares, "is different...it has got me hooked personally. I got to live it, from the inside." Muttering that Horton is a "damn fool," the publisher finally relents.

On the road, Horton encounters hate and hurt from whites. He is bullied by a sadistic bus driver; chased and terrorized by young toughs; and discriminated against by employers ("We're gradually weeding you people out," a plant manager says). The white men who give him rides in their cars feel free to question him about his sex life. "Ever have a white woman?" one leeringly asks. While the book contains a few such episodes, they recur so often in the film that it turns into a kind of verbal porn flick.

The humiliation Horton suffers as a black in a white man's country causes him to lose track of who he is. Near the end of his journey, he visits a Catholic church and pours out his anguish to the priest. "Father," he says, "since I started, something has happened to me that I had not foreseen. It horrifies me. It's as though I were no longer myself. I look like a stranger, I live like a stranger. Now I'm beginning to feel like a stranger. It's as though I had lost my immortal soul."

> **Priest:** "You cannot lose your immortal soul.... What you have lost is your pride of self."
>
> **Horton:** "Everything I've done, I've done for brotherhood. How can self enter into it?"
>
> **Priest:** "On this journey, your goal was... ?"
>
> **Horton:** "To see how it was to be a Negro in the South. Maritain said, 'To prepare a new age of the world, martyrs to the love of neighbors must first be necessary.' Those words were like a command to me. Now I find myself acting like an inferior colored man."
>
> **Priest:** "An inferior colored man?"
>
> **Horton:** "That, too, has happened to me. I'm filled with prejudice, Father. It's like a poison. I thought I had purged myself, but I had not."

The priest, seeking to end their session on a positive note, assures Horton, "When you return home, my son, you'll be stronger for the ordeal you've gone through." But that is more platitude than guarantee. Neither black nor white appreciates what Horton has done. A young black man, a fiery freedom rider to whom the reporter has confided his real identity, explodes: "And now you know what it's like [to be black]? After ten weeks or three months or whatever, you know?" He gives a short, derisive laugh at the absurdity of it. His old father apologizes for the outburst, then asks, "The white folks that read this, the folks back home, they'll believe you, won't they, now that they know how it is?" Horton's answer is a curious mixture of defiance and doubt. "I don't know that," he says, "I don't know that at all.... All I know is, I'll tell them."

In the closing scene, Horton wanders, suitcase in hand, down the sun-blistered streets of a poor black neighborhood. The faces of the people he has met on his journey—cruel white faces, hopeless black faces—flash through his mind. He crosses the white dividing line of a highway, symbol of the color bar and of the split within himself. His attempt to understand how the other half lives has brought him only torment. The truth doesn't necessarily set you free; it may drive you crazy with guilt and grief.

*The Parallax View,* directed by Alan Pakula and adapted by David Gilder and Lorenzo Semple, Jr. from a novel by Loren Singer, is about the way perspective can be manipulated to hide the truth. According to the dictionary, "parallax" means "the apparent displacement of an observed object due to a change in the position of the observer." Or "the difference between the view of an object as seen through the picture-taking lens of a camera and the view as seen through a separate viewfinder."

Drawing plot details from the killings of John and Robert Kennedy, the film opens with the shooting of charismatic Senator Carroll in Seattle's Space Needle. A government commission hands down a report saying the assassination was the work of a lone gunman. But after seven witnesses to the crime die under suspicious circumstances, journalist Joe Frady (Warren Beatty) decides to investigate. He uncovers the Parallax Corporation, which hires out assassins to anyone who can pay. To penetrate the conspiracy, he offers himself as a recruit. His hunt ends with another political murder and, more startlingly, his own destruction.

Critical opinion on *The Parallax View* was sharply divided. Many reviewers thought the film reckless for suggesting that the assassinations of the sixties could have been arranged by a secret group. "Though a touch of paranoid fantasizing can energize an entertainment," Richard Schickel of *Time* commented, "too much of it is just plain crazy—neither truthful nor useful. And certainly nothing to try to make a buck with in the movies."[31] Stephen Farber, in the *New York Times,* called *The Parallax View* the "most mindless and irresponsible" of the conspiracy films that sprang up after the Watergate revelations. "Today's mass audience," he complained, "wants to believe in omnipotent, omniscient, indestructible conspiracies." He said the possibility that the course of history could be changed by a freak accident was just too disturbing for the public to contemplate.[32]

Joseph Kanon agreed in *Atlantic* that *The Parallax View*

"marks a new, and rather chilling, shift in popular movies," but didn't wax indignant about the development. "[T]he stuff of suspense thrillers," he pointed out, "has entered the mainstream of national life. *The Parallax View* and *The Conversation* [about an expert in electronic surveillance who is victimized by his own expertise] are probably the most 'seventies' movies of the year because they dig at our preoccupations and turn the panic of the sixties' random violence into a more organized, contemporary menace. We don't have to believe in conspiracies to feel the mental climate that produced them."[33]

Young, shaggy-haired Frady doesn't believe in conspiracies, at least not in the beginning. When his ex-girlfriend (Paula Prentiss), a TV correspondent who witnessed the Carroll assassination, comes to him in tears and insists, "Somebody is trying to kill me," he refuses to take

Investigative reporter Joe Frady (Warren Beatty) is trapped by a murderous conspiracy in the climactic scene of *The Parallax View.*

her seriously. But the next time he sees her, she is a body in the morgue. His suspicion aroused, he prepares to go undercover. He asks a private-eye acquaintance to provide him with an alias and an ID.

> **Detective:** "What kind of an ID?"
>
> **Frady:** "Got to be a hostile misfit."
>
> **Detective:** "For that, you don't need an ID."

The wisecrack is revealing. Frady doesn't wholly belong to straight society, and his ambiguous status allows him heroic freedom of thought and action. As an outcast, he is unencumbered by conventional wisdom, is willing and able to make connections others can't or won't. He is that central figure of American mythology, the frontiersman, living by his wits and his own code in the margin between the dark forest and civilization.

His search brings him first to the small rustic town of Salmontail. Its folksy sheriff turns out to be a member of the conspiracy and tries to drown him. If the law has been suborned, shysters and savages will reign unless a loyal individual or institution steps into the breach and assumes authority. The transfer of guardianship is visually accented when Frady escapes in a patrol car, wearing the sheriff's white cowboy hat.

Returning late at night to the newspaper office, Frady outlines for his crusty old editor (Hume Cronyn) a wild tale of a national assassination bureau. "You've been drinking again, haven't you?" the editor accuses, and adds: "I don't care if your self-serving ambition gets you a paperback sale *and* the Pulitzer Prize [à la Watergate investigators Bob Woodward and Carl Bernstein, then at the height of their fame]. I'm not going to have any more to do with it." He softens after another attempt is made on Frady's life, but still can't help skeptically exclaiming, "You're telling me that you alone can uncover what all these agencies couldn't?"

The viewer is led to believe that this is precisely what

Frady can do. Although the Parallax Corporation has a long reach, the reporter keeps wriggling out of its grasp—until the film's final moments. A politician is assassinated at the Los Angeles convention center. Frady, trapped in the hall's shadowy rafters, realizes that he has been set up. He flees through a maze of ramps and corridors, then sees an open door and sprints toward it. The silhouette of a man with a shotgun suddenly fills the lighted space, and Frady is blasted. "It's a staggering climax," Kanon wrote, "not only because we've invested so much emotion in the hero or because we're surprised at the terrible logic, but because it violates all our *movie* expectations."[34] The happy ending, the benediction that years of moviegoing has conditioned us to expect, never materializes.

Instead a high tribunal, photographed with a wide-angle lens and surrounded by darkness, issues a report attributing the politician's death to a mad assassin: Frady. The journalist's best qualities—his curiosity, his dogged-

Taggart (Ryan O'Neal, second from left), a sportswriter investigating the nether world of gambling, becomes a compulsive gambler himself in *Fever Pitch.*

ness, his nonconformity—are taken as evidence of "a confused and distorted mind." While Frady succeeded in entering the labyrinth, he could find no exit. The film leaves the viewer feeling similarly cornered. For if a Hollywood star with all the magic of the movies at his disposal can't escape the monster, what chance have we?

Taggart (Ryan O'Neal), sports reporter for the *Los Angeles Herald Examiner* in Richard Brooks' *Fever Pitch,* is being devoured by a monster of his own creation. The film opens with his arrival in Las Vegas to wrap up an investigative series on gambling. He has sunk to the desperate level of the losers and grifters he writes about. In trying to get to know them, and "how it feels to live on the edge," he has become a compulsive gambler himself, the pseudonymous "Mr. Green" mentioned in his articles.

But Taggart has lost more than a lot of money; he also has lost his wife. She, it is revealed in a melodramatic and clumsy flashback, was killed in a car crash while rushing to bail him out of a jam with a bookie. He still owes $31,000 to "The Dutchman" (Chad Everett), who menacingly refers to the reporter's young daughter as "the only collateral you've got."

Despite his clean-cut Boy Scout looks, and his occasional Boy Scout morality (in an early scene, he rejects the favors of a showgirl-prostitute), Taggart is out of control. He lies, drinks heavily, and eventually lands in jail. After hitting bottom with a thud, he joins Gamblers Anonymous. The picture might have ended there, with Taggart struggling to come to terms with his addiction. But writer-director Brooks spares him the bother. In an improbable comic coda, Taggart has a streak of luck at the gaming tables and wins enough to pay off his debts.

Until then, *Fever Pitch* portrays the investigative reporter as a victim of his own charade. Taggart is changed and corrupted by the false role he lives. "Which one is you?" his editor (John Saxon) wonders upon belatedly learning that "Mr. Green" is a pseudonym for the reporter. "I don't know," Taggart admits. With the heroes of *Black Like Me* and *The Parallax View,* he enters so convincingly into an impersonation that his sense of self vanishes.

All the reporters go too far. They tamper with a mystery of the universe and tempt cosmic retribution. The films recall myths and fairy tales that describe the special traps and revenges lying in wait for those who would violate secrets: "[s]ilent forests that frighten and yet allure; sealed caves entrusted to the charge of spirits; beckoning sirens whose promises of delight cause sailors to perish; realms of the dead where to look backward is to be turned to stone...."[35] The oppressive climate of the films may be immediately traceable to the public crises of the sixties and seventies, but more darkly, it reflects an atavastic fear that there are some secrets too awful to investigate, and that the penalty for uncovering them is madness or death.

## *The Investigative Reporter As Comedian:* Continental Divide *(1981),* Perfect *(1985), and* Fletch *(1985).*

It must be fun being a reporter nowadays.—Jessie Wilson, *Perfect*

The most memorable newspaper films of the thirties and forties are comedies. In fact, they may be the most memorable newspaper films, period. Whenever I confided to someone that I was writing a book on the image of journalists in film—and I am afraid that I confided it about as often as I could—the person would begin naming movies. Top mentions were *The Front Page* (1931), *It Happened One Night* (1934), and *His Girl Friday* (1940). Reporters are associated in a lot of people's minds more with one-liners than bylines.

And for good reason. The Hollywood reporter was issued a quick, mordant wit along with his first press pass. He expressed his disdain for conventional values in a steady stream of wisecracks. It was his defense against co-optation by a corrupt, shallow society. "Oh, you're such a smart aleck," heiress Ellen Andrews (Claudette Colbert) says in exasperation to newspaperman Peter Warne (Clark Gable) in Frank Capra's *It Happened One Night.* "Nobody knows anything but you." What he knows is that she and her glittering friends are, as he democratically puts it, "a lot of hooey." His repartee is the great leveler, cutting the powerful and pompous down to human size or even smaller.

The hero and heroine of newspaper comedies start out at swords' points, but wind up in each others' arms. "If you got any silly notion that I'm interested in you," Peter snaps at Ellen, who is running away to New York on an overnight bus, "forget it. You're just a headline to me." By the last shot, she is his wife. *It Happened One Night,* the first picture to sweep all four major Academy Awards, inspired a wave of "screwball comedies" in the thirties, and it is still being cloned. The copies celebrate the wonder of love and the promise of democracy by magically uniting social opposites: a city editor who graduated from the "school of hard knocks" and a prissy journalism professor in *Teacher's Pet* (1958); a TV correspondent and a drunken rodeo cowboy in *Electric Horseman* (1979); a Chicago columnist and an ornithologist in *Continental Divide;* a *Rolling Stone* reporter and an aerobics instructor in *Perfect;* a detective reporter and—who else?—an heiress in *Fletch.*

Certain scenes and visual details are repeated from movie to movie with only slight variation. After their bus drives off the road in a blinding rain, Peter and Ellen are forced to share a tourist cabin (he registers them, in a bit of foreshadowing, as husband and wife). She is reluctant to sleep in the same room with him, but he hangs a blanket on a clothesline between the beds to reassure her of his honorable intentions. The blanket, which he jokingly refers to as the "walls of Jericho," symbolizes the class and other barriers that separate them. On their actual wedding night, he blows a toy trumpet, and the walls come tumbling down. *Continental Divide,* directed by Michael Apted and written by Lawrence Kasdan, uses a similar device to convey the initial distance between naturalist Nell Porter (Blair Brown) and journalist Ernie Souchak (John Belushi). Every time she steps into the doorless shower in her log cabin, he has to step outside. And just as Peter makes Ellen breakfast in a sequence that is both a parody and projection of domestic bliss, Ernie cooks Nell goulash according to his grandmother's recipe. It is all part of an elaborate mating ritual.

Significantly, *The Front Page,* the prototype for the anti-press film, reverses this narrative formula. It begins with Hildy Johnson's impending marriage and proceeds to throw obstacles between the crime reporter and his bride-to-be. The last shot doesn't show Hildy and Peggy in a clinch, but that "double-crossing maniac" Walter Burns phoning the police. "The son of a bitch stole my watch," he says of Hildy, an audacious ruse to prevent the reporter from leaving town. Rather than promising a new, more cohesive society, the ending promises a new cycle of chaos.

Modern newspaper comedies with a romantic bent are exercises in nostalgia. On the surface, they may seem relentlessly up to date, reflecting the latest fantasies and fads, whether bean sprouts or male strippers. Sex isn't graphically depicted, but it is frequent, and the language can be raw. "Wanna fuck?" aerobics teacher Jessie Wilson (Jamie Lee Curtis) types on reporter Adam Lawrence's (John Travolta) portable computer in *Perfect.* Nonetheless, Aaron Latham, the former *Rolling Stone* writer who did the screenplay, said he and director James Bridges intended the movie as a throwback to the romantic journalism comedies of the thirties.[36] Good old-fashioned monogamy would be enshrined as the answer to most of life's problems.

*Perfect* and the smoother *Continental Divide* offer psychic balm to the casualties of the Sexual Revolution. The couples in these films resolve the conflict between romance and sex, or between marriage and a career, without spilling too much blood. Both Ernie and Adam are happily married to their jobs when the viewer first sees them. Neither is prepared for what follows. Ernie gets his face rearranged by hoods for muckraking a corrupt alderman, and his editor (Allen Goorwitz) orders him to Wyoming to do a story on Nell until things cool down. Born and bred in the city, he doesn't relish the prospect of visiting the Rockies. "Fresh air makes me nauseous," he says. Adam, in contrast, looks forward to writing about the health-club craze.

"It'll be hilarious, particularly set in Los Angeles," he tells his editor (played by Jann Wenner, the real-life editor of *Rolling Stone*). "You know, inflated bodies, airheads. . . ." His eagerness and Ernie's cantankerousness turn out to be two sides of the same irony, the irony of a tough, arrogant reporter finding love where he expects to find just another story.

In each film, boy meets girl—and a lot of resistance. Nell despises the peeping tomism of the press and won't agree to an interview. "There's nothing personal in this . . . ," she explains to Ernie. "But I do serious work here, in private and in peace. I'm not a pop singer. I don't have a million records to sell. Publicity is trite and trivial. Reporters are parasites, living off the accomplishments of other people. I don't see newspapers much, but what I see sickens me." "Well," Ernie responds, "they only cost 20

*Rolling Stone* reporter Adam Lawrence (John Travolta) goes behind the scenes for a trendy article on health clubs in *Perfect.*

Ornithologist Nell Porter (Blair Brown) and Chicago columnist Ernie Souchak (John Belushi) are the odd couple in *Continental Divide.*

cents." It is a riposte worthy of his sardonic forefathers, the ink-stained wags of *The Front Page.*

Adam goes through a shorter, less funny, but otherwise identical routine with Jessie. "Give me a reason why," he demands after she refuses to be interviewed. "I read magazines," she says.

The reporters, who cultivate a macho style, must be sensitized by the women, initiated into mysteries of the heart, before suspicion can give way to love. "Understand nature...," Nell urges Ernie, and adds: "If you want to tame or conquer anything, you got to understand what it's like to be the object of that conquest, and that applies whether it's an eagle or a stream or me." Jessie has a similar line. Stunned to hear Adam describe an interview as a "seduction," she warns, "I think anything worthwhile takes longer—working out, a relationship."

Falling in love complicates all their lives. "I'm glad that I met you," Jessie says to Adam, "and I'm sorry that I met you." In *Continental Divide,* there is a lyrical piece of dialogue, reminiscent of Walt Whitman's poem "The Dalliance of the Eagles," that serves as a metaphor for the hero and heroine's contradictory impulses to join together and to flee one another. Ernie has returned to Chicago, his column, and exposing corruption, and seemingly has forgotten Nell, when she shows up in the city to deliver a lecture. He can't stay away and, in the question-and-answer period that follows, coyly asks how eagles make love.

> **Nell:** "First they chase each other, circling, dipping, twisting, screaming, testing."
>
> **Ernie:** "And then?"
>
> **Nell:** "Then they come together, their talons locking."
>
> **Ernie:** "Inseparable?"
>
> **Nell:** "For a short, very happy time."
>
> **Ernie:** "And they fly that way?"
>
> **Nell:** "No, not together. They begin to fall, tumbling and plunging down and down."
>
> **Ernie:** "Oh, it sounds dangerous."
>
> **Nell:** "Yes, but thrilling."
>
> **Ernie:** "And then?"
>
> **Nell:** "And then, when they're very near the ground—"
>
> **Ernie:** "About to be smashed."
>
> **Nell:** "—they separate, open their wings, and soar on the air currents."
>
> **Ernie:** "Alone?"

**Nell:** "Each alone, that's the only way they can fly."

**Ernie:** "And that's all there is?"

**Nell:** "Unless they do it again."

Nell and Ernie do it again ... and again ... and again, for they get married. And why shouldn't they tie the knot, since it is a slip knot? They plan to maintain separate careers and lifestyles; their marriage involves no sacrifice or compromise on either's part. "I'll see you when the snow melts," Nell sings out as Ernie leaps on a train for Chicago at the end of the picture. Jessie and Adam also find harmony after numerous scrapes and squabbles. He writes a dirty-minded piece, "Looking for Mr. Goodbody," that portrays health clubs as the "single bars of the eighties." She reads a draft of it and upbraids him ("You're so disgusting," she says). He feels guilty and rewrites the story. The magazine publishes the original sensational version. He flies to Morocco on assignment. He flies home and wrecks the editor's office with a baseball bat. He goes to jail (not for wrecking the office, but for refusing to reveal his sources for yet another story). He gets out of jail. A forgiving Jessie—and a pack of reporters and photographers—are waiting for him. Hero and heroine kiss and drive off into the sunset in a BMW (the fantasy wouldn't be complete if the car were a Ford).

The aim of both *Perfect* and *Continental Divide* isn't to air issues, but to smother them. The films seem nicely calculated to appeal to those brought up on the notion that they can have it all—great sex and good careers, a loving, photogenic family and personal freedom. If what most people have instead are messy divorces or frustrating jobs or rebellious kids, it may render the dream world on the screen only that much more necessary and alluring.

*Fletch* was dismissed by a lot of critics—prematurely, I think—as simple escapist entertainment. Jack Kroll of *Newsweek* said it is "such soft fare that it makes your eyes feel gummy," while Vincent Canby of the *New York Times* called it "an enjoyable paperback of a film, a lightweight, breezy experience.... "[37] Actually, the film, directed by

Michael Ritchie and adapted by Andrew Bergman from a novel by Gregory McDonald, is wildly satirical and wholly subversive. "Everything a joke to you, Fletch?" Fat Sam (George Wendt), a dope dealer, asks. "Everything," confirms the smart-alecky reporter (Chevy Chase), serious for once.

The film opens with Fletch posing as an "amiable, minor-league junkie" to investigate the drug traffic on a Los Angeles-area beach. Later he introduces himself to sources as Gordon Liddy, Don Corleone, Arnold Babar (as in the elephant), Harry S Truman, Igor Stravinsky, Mr. Poon of the Security and Exchange Commission (Question: "What kind of name is Poon?" Answer: "Comanche Indian."), and Dr. Rosenpenis. The reporters in *Black Like Me, The Parallax View,* and *Fever Pitch* are imprisoned in their false roles, but Fletch changes identities the way a nymphomaniac changes sex partners. His endless charade

Detective reporter Irwin Fletcher (Chevy Chase) masquerades as a waiter to elude corrupt police in *Fletch.*

is an ironic reflection of fluid, fast-paced American culture, with its instant celebrities and disposable lifestyles, its possibilities for remaking oneself in almost any image with the purchase of the right clothes or car, its temptations for social climbing, selling out, and fraud.

Status symbols and authority figures are present primarily to be chewed up, Fletcherized. Rehearsing his tennis swing as he walks through the parking lot of a country club, Fletch accidentally smashes a Mercedes Benz with his racket, an act that would have been tantamount to sacrilege in *Perfect.* When a corrupt police chief (Joe Don Baker) asks, "What do you do for a living, Mr. Fletch?", he replies, "I'm a shepherd." Hounded by his editor (Richard Libertini) for "something to print," he sticks up his middle finger and says, "Print this."

For all the film's rowdiness, its plot is a classic one of hard-boiled detective fiction. Fletch discovers that Police Chief Karlin controls the drug trade on the beach, and that Stanwyck (Tim Matheson), a wealthy young business executive, is a bigamist as well as dope smuggler. It is a vision of institutionalized corruption and perverted passion familiar to devotees of Raymond Chandler and Ross Macdonald, whose novels portray Southern California as a lost paradise of faded blondes and dime-store dreams, of cops on the take and shadows on the soul. Like Chandler's Philip Marlowe and Macdonald's Lew Archer, Fletch is a lonely crusader, a tired rumpled knight, vulnerable behind his shield of wisecracks. He challenges evildoers and rescues a damsel in distress—Stanwyck's wife, Gail (Dana Wheeler-Nicholson)—partly because that is his job, but more importantly, because his unspoken code requires it.

The ending suggests a society on the mend, no longer haunted by killers and crooks. "The coroner certified Stanwyck dead—or extremely sleepy," Fletch narrates, "and Chief Karlin was facing twenty years in the funhouse. I decided to accompany Gail to Rio and personally assist her in her grief therapy." This is a pretty fair description of what the newspaper comedies of the 1980s do on a broader scale: assist viewers in their "grief therapy." Surveying the cultural tumult of the past two decades, Thomas Hine wrote, "The American Way of Life has shattered into a bewildering array of 'lifestyles,' which offer greater freedom but not the security that one is doing the normal thing."[38] The films address our loss of certainty and direction, and compensate for it by showing us heroes and heroines who somehow integrate their divergent backgrounds, professions and values, and find romance. We are asked to put our faith in the fantasy that good triumphs, that time heals all hurts, that the kissing never stops. And who can blame us if we do?

## *The Investigative Reporter As Penitent:* The Odessa File *(1974),* The China Syndrome *(1979),* The Year of the Dragon *(1985), and* A Flash of Green *(1985)*

> Nothing is more American than optimism accompanied by a pervasive sense of dread.—Ruth Rosen, "Search for Yesterday"

*The Odessa File* is a thriller, and *The China Syndrome* a "monster movie," with technology, as its director, James Bridges, said, the monster.[39] *A Flash of Green* is a stylized, kabuki-like morality tale, and *The Year of the Dragon* a sort of urban Western ("There's a new marshall in town—me," its policeman hero announces). Yet the differences among the films are finally less striking than the similarities. All treat to one degree or other the spiritual redemption of a reporter.

Early in *The Odessa File,* directed by Ronald Neame and based on Frederick Forsythe's best seller, the girlfriend of German free-lancer Peter Miller (Jon Voight) bursts out: "You're a parasite. You live off other people's troubles." But he sees himself as a "pro," doing his job the best way he knows how. "I like my work," he says. "I'm conscientious and ambitious." Then he stumbles on a story that curdles his rampant professionalism. An old Jew commits suicide, leaving behind a diary that chronicles the horrors of the Nazi concentration camps, and that hints at the existence of a secret society of former SS men, the "Odessa" of the title. After poring over the dairy, and absorbing its cry of pain, Miller launches a one-man crusade to avenge the Jew's death and expose the war criminals.

He pursues the investigation against all advice. "People don't want to know . . . ," an editor tells him. "It's a dead duck." A police source urges, "Leave it alone, Peter, please." Even his supposedly humane girlfriend says, "Who cares [about the death camps]?" "I care," he yells. "I'm feeling a sense of responsibility." A reporter with a nose for a possible scoop becomes, by default, society's conscience.

Miller owes no loyalty to any employer or organization. As a free lance, he belongs to himself and contends in a cause of his own choosing. In *The Odessa File*—and in *The China Syndrome* and *A Flash of Green,* too—the truth is dug up by a renegade reporter, not the institution of the press. The journalistic establishment is part of a larger corrupt Establishment. Its interests mesh with those of a varied collection of villains, from real-estate developers and utility companies to crime lords and neo-Nazis.

Paranoia about far-reaching conspiracies is particularly marked in *The Odessa File.* At the beginning of the film, Miller hears on his car radio that President Kennedy has been assassinated. The shooting isn't remotely connected to the plot, but mention of it sets a mood of pervasive menace. "Odessa" itself is described as "growing like a spider's web" and as having "penetrated every facet of life": commerce, the courts, police. Yet Miller, empowered by his righteous wrath (and screenwriters Kenneth Ross and George Markstein), still prevails over the conspirators in the end.

As this synopsis suggests, films that cast an investigative reporter in the role of fanatical penitent lie close to the axis of the journalism film genre. The story pattern shares with the anti-press films a harsh view of the news business. At the same time, it resembles the war correspondent films in charting the moral development of a reporter. No other narrative seems so flexible, holds so many polarities in precarious balance: rugged individualism and its underside of atomism; the community as a sink of corruption and communal life as the source of identity and

Kimberly Wells (Jane Fonda), who was hired by a Los Angeles TV station for her looks and not her investigative abilities, finally gets the chance to do some real reporting in *The China Syndrome*.

meaning; the evil of cold professionalism and the need for professional cool in rooting out evil. It is an incredible acrobatic feat, like a pyramid of elephants—on a skateboard.

*The China Syndrome* massages most of these tensions. Directed by James Bridges and written by Bridges, T.S. Cook, and Mike Gray, the film concerns an accident at a nuclear power plant in California and the fallout for a TV reporter. Much about *The China Syndrome* was controversial, even the title. It is jargon for a reactor meltdown that could, theoretically, burn through steel, through concrete, through earth to China. Columbia Pictures worried that the title would mystify the public and thought of changing it to *Eyewitness* or *Power.*[40] Meanwhile, the energy industry worried that the film, by any name, would hurt its image. Half of the January/February 1979 issue of *Reddy News,* a trade magazine, was devoted to an attack on *The China Syndrome.* "Just in case you don't have enough grief," the article warned, "this 'contemporary thriller' will open in your service area March 16."[41] If there is a lesson here, it is that journalists aren't alone in feeling persecuted by Hollywood.

Fate, however, played a singularly cruel trick on the advocates of nuclear power. Twelve days after *The China Syndrome* opened to generally favorable reviews and strong business at the box office, the worst nuclear accident in the nation's history occurred at the Three Mile Island plant in Harrisburg, Pennsylvania. The accident focused additional attention on the film, which became the biggest non-holiday hit Columbia had ever had.[42] The film was, in *Newsweek's* words, "that rare phenomenon—a piece of popular entertainment that immediately foreshadows a major news event and then helps explain it."[43] In the eeriest coincidence, a physicist in the film claims that a meltdown in California could "render an area the size of Pennsylvania permanently uninhabitable."

Although nuclear power was the most topical issue in *The China Syndrome,* it portrayed another technology as equally ominous: TV. Jane Fonda stars as Kimberly Wells, a former actress in commercials who does soft news for a

Los Angeles station. She wants to try "some real reporting," but management opposes the idea. "[Y]ou didn't get this job because of your investigative abilities," news director Don Jacovich (Peter Donat) reminds her.

"Journalists are writers of stories," James Carey noted, "and, after hours, tellers of stories as well. The stories they tell are of stories they got, stories they scooped, and cautionary little tales that educate the apprentice to the glories, dangers, mysteries, and desires of the craft."[44] Kimberly and her crew happen on the mythical "big story"—the one that brings shouts of "Stop the presses!" in old movies—while doing an innocuous feature on the Ventana Nuclear Power Plant. A strange rumbling triggers panic in the control room. Her cameraman, Richard Adams (Michael Douglas), a radical leftover from the sixties, secretly films the "event"—nuclear slang for a near meltdown. This is the first decent story the station has had in months, but Jacovich, wary of a lawsuit, refuses to air it.

Richard charges a "goddamn cover-up." He is shocked and disgusted when Kimberly doesn't react with similar heat. "So you're just going to sit here?" he explodes. "This is it?" Jacovich answers for her: "It's none of her business. She doesn't make policy. She's a performer, a professional." To be a professional, then, means to submit to neutering, to become, as Richard says of Kimberly, a "piece of walking furniture." Richard is the reporter's virtuous alter ego, like Kwan in *The Year of Living Dangerously* (1983) or Christine in *The Mean Season* (1984). His constant criticism of Kimberly's go-along-to-get-along attitude, and her own eagerness to cover something more substantial than a birthday party for a tiger at the zoo, eventually combine to push her into taking a moral stand.

A parallel course is traveled by Jack Godell (Jack Lemmon), a shift supervisor at the plant. After a government commission whitewashes the "event," he launches a probe of his own and finds that safety records have been falsified. Utility officials, warped by greed, ignore his warnings about the chance of a catastrophic accident. The construction company that built the plant sends thugs to kill him. He tries to pass his evidence to Kimberly, but the go-between is ambushed. Down to his last desperate option, Godell seizes a gun from a security guard at the plant and takes over the control room.

He demands that Kimberly be allowed to interview him. A tense sequence follows in which a SWAT team dashes up one flight of stairs, a camera team up another. The SWAT team wins the race. They machine-gun Godell before Kimberly's horrified eyes. Then the control room begins to rumble and shake, and the lights go out. The catastrophe Godell feared is only narrowly averted.

Within minutes, a spokesman for the utility is addressing the media in front of the plant. "The public was never in any danger at any time," he says. He describes Godell as "emotionally unstable" and possibly drunk—shades of *The Parallax View.* TV cameras grind away, and print reporters dutifully jot down quotes. Suddenly Kimberly appears and challenges the cover-up. She asks a co-worker of Godell's (Wilford Brimley), who has been brought forward by the spokesman, if the slain supervisor had reason to be alarmed, if the plant is unsafe and should be closed. The worker stonewalls, but Kimberly keeps hammering at him, and, finally, he cracks. "There will be an investigation this time," he predicts. "The truth will come out. People will know Jack Godell wasn't a loony, he was a hero."

Kimberly turns a strained, tear-streaked face toward a Minicam. "I'm sorry I'm not very objective," she tells the home audience. "Let's just hope it doesn't end here." Back at the studio, Jacovich has been watching her live report on a monitor. "She did a helluva good job," he declares, and adds, with irrepressible hypocrisy: "I must say I'm not surprised."

*The China Syndrome* recoils from the absolute blackness of *The Parallax View.* Kimberly seems to grow in professional stature, and good seems to triumph. Yet the victory over greed, if victory is what it is, feels curiously tentative, almost ironic. Jacovich, who is scarcely less of an ogre, though a bit more of an oaf, than the head of the utility, emerges from the battle with his power intact. He is, like his medium, impervious. All images on TV are created equal—equally banal. Broadcast between a game show and a singing commercial for microwave ovens, Kimberly's report is but a fragment, a moment, in an ever-shifting kaleidoscope of moments, each as flashy, and forgettable, as the next.

Godell dies for our sins (his name may allude to the Supreme Shift Supervisor). Nothing so drastic is required of Kimberly. She only has to lose her self-possession and cry on camera, and even then she earns points with the boss. From Jacovich's "bottom-line, dollar-sign" perspective, her tearful plea is another gimmick for holding the attention of jaded TV viewers.[45] *The China Syndrome* is remarkable for how smoothly it strokes both our hopes and phobias. It appeals to our wishfulness by promising that truth will out, while it confirms our dread by insinuating that such a promise is vainglorious.

Compared with a sleek thriller like *The China Syndrome,* writer-director Michael Cimino's *The Year of the Dragon* is a big roaring drunk of a movie. The characters are always shouting at each other or shooting at each other. Stanley White (Mickey Rourke), the film's uncompromising hero, is a Vietnam veteran (Oliver Stone of *Platoon* fame co-wrote the script) and the most decorated cop in the history of the New York City Police Department. He has been assigned to clean up the youth gangs preying on merchants in Chinatown. Not one to tolerate evil—or, for that matter, civil liberties—he exceeds his orders and wages all-out war on the Chinese Triads, a shadowy criminal organization that predates the Mafia.

White wants to enlist TV reporter Tracy Tzu, played by the model Ariane, in his crusade. First he tries flattery: "I think you're pretty good. A helluva lot sexier than the broads on the other channels." When that gets him nowhere, he tries bribery: "Look, I'll give you hard facts off the record. You do one of those exposés on Chinatown. One week you do the gambling connection.... Work the way up the ladder to the bosses. You splash their faces on the tube. Take a little journalistic license. You know what I mean." Indeed, she does and is outraged. "There are

Police captain Stanley White (Mickey Rourke) breaks egg rolls with reporter Tracy Tzu (Ariane) in a Chinatown restaurant in *The Year of the Dragon*.

boundaries, White, ethics," she fumes. "The press is independent. It's not just another undercover cop."

He changes her mind in a revolting scene. Arriving uninvited at her lavish Manhattan loft—its lavishness suggests that she is more a celebrity and sybarite than a serious journalist—he launches into a rant against the press: "You wanna know what's destroying this country? It's not booze, it's not drugs. It's TV, it's media, it's people like you, vampires. I hate the way you lie every night at 6 o'clock. I hate the way you kill real feeling. I hate everything you stand for." Foreplay is now over. He forces himself on her, and his brutality makes her love him. White—talk about symbolic names!—is an evangelist of the "White Man's Burden," aggression hopped up and hallowed, America dispensing democracy to the black, brown, and yellow races, to Vietnam, Cambodia, El Salvador, and Nicaragua, with screaming bombs, a rhapsody of blood and death. To round things off, Tracy is later gang-raped by young

Chinese punks in retaliation for helping White. The figurative rape of reporter Megan Carter in *Absence of Malice* (1981) is literalized here, and not once, but twice. The film is about as subtle as a dog in heat.

Pauline Kael pronounced Cimino and Stone's "one of the tawdriest and stupidest scripts that could ever have been put into production as a major film."[46] Robert Daley, author of the novel on which the script was based, sent copies of his book to journalists, asking them to read it before, or instead of, seeing the film version. Asian-Americans complained about the film's racist overtones and picketed theaters showing it in New York, Boston, Los Angeles, and other cities. MGM/UA finally added a disclaimer to *The Year of the Dragon,* which said in part: "This film does not intend to demean or to ignore the many positive features of Asian-Americans and specifically Chinese-American communities."[47]

*A Flash of Green* is a much quieter film—so quiet, in fact, that its release went largely unnoticed. Directed by Victor Nunez, who adapted the script from a novel by John D. MacDonald, it is set in Palm City on the west coast of Florida around 1960. Ed Harris plays Jimmy Wing, reporter for the *Record-Journal.* He covers highway smash-ups, meetings, child drownings, and the dedication in a trailer park of a bronze plaque commemorating the "Heroes of the Red Peril." Wing is talented enough to work for a first-class paper. He remains in Palm City because his wife is hospitalized, dying of a degenerative nerve disease, and because it is his hometown, and there is no place like home.

But home could wind up like a lot of other places, overbuilt and overrun, if land developers win approval to dredge Grassy Bay. Elmo Bliss (Richard Jordan), a boyhood friend of Wing's and a county commissioner with ambitions to be governor, is the driving force behind the ecologically disastrous scheme. "The world needs folks like me," Bliss says at one point, "folks with a raw need for power." He offers Wing a bribe in exchange for supplying information that can be used to blackmail members of a "Save Our Bay" group. The reporter's motives for accepting the money are never fully explained. There is an air of inevitability about his fall from grace and his repentance and salvation.

From the moment Wing takes the first payoff, his conscience nags at him. And when he sees the insane extremes to which Bliss will go—an opponent of the project, a woman, is tied to a tree and flogged—he decides to expose the conspiracy, including his own role in it. The paper has touted the developers and suppressed news about the environmentalists, but one night Wing manages to smuggle onto the front page the sensational story of bribery and spying and hooliganism. "You sure made a helluva mess out of a simple real-estate transaction," a lawyer later tells him.

Wing actually suffers more than the deal does. He is fired from the paper. His wife dies. Kat Hubble (Blair Brown), his best friend's widow and the woman he loves, rejects him. Bliss' goons stomp him. He could go away and leave Palm City to its corruption. Instead he stays and deeply atones by embracing his outcast status. His presence reminds the morally tainted community of what it wants to forget. He becomes a sort of embarrassing municipal monument to the big crimes that pass for progress in the small town.

Films that portray a reporter as a recovering sinner are usually rife with contradictions and ambiguities. *A Flash of Green* is no exception. Wing gets back his job, and he and Kat are reconciled, but Grassy Bay is filled in, and the beauty of wild things lost forever. The very title of the film has a double meaning. The green flash refers, obviously, to the dazzle of money. But it also refers to a phenomenon that takes place on Florida's west coast only when the horizon is absolutely free of haze. As the upper rim of the setting sun disappears beneath the Gulf of Mexico, there can occur, for a fraction of a second, a brilliant emerald illumination of the entire sky, an explosion of light so brief you can't be sure you really saw it.[48] Although if you did, and quickly made a wish, they say it will come true.

## *The Investigative Reporter As Knight Without Armor:* All the President's Men *(1976)*

> There's no question, however, that the investigative reporter has become—rather like the foreign correspondent in his trenchcoat used to be—the most idealized and romanticized figure in journalism today. —Tom Wicker, *On Press*

Last semester I showed *All the President's Men* to my beginning reporting class. The students were mostly freshman and sophomores, 18- and 19-year-olds. I wasn't much older than them when I saw the film for the first time. Their reaction was strange. They laughed. They laughed at the bungling of the Watergate burglars. They laughed at the fatigue of Bob Woodward (Robert Redford) as he sat at his desk in the *Washington Post* newsroom and worked the phone hour after tedious hour to track down a source. They laughed at the transparent lies and evasions of the officials taking part in the White House cover-up. I show a film about the greatest constitutional crisis in modern American history, and my students laugh their heads off!

I had been something of a Watergate junkie—I also said "Outta sight!" a lot, marched against the Vietnam War, and voted for McGovern—while the scandal was unfolding. I had pored over the stories in the paper with the avidity of an archeologist poring over precious fragments of an ancient manuscript. I had followed the Senate Watergate hearings on TV the way housewives and shut-ins follow afternoon soap operas. I had read Woodward and Carl Bernstein's book about the cover-up as soon as it was published, and I had seen the film version as soon as it was released. At the time—a time of disillusion and doubt—*All the President's Men* had seemed to me chillingly real. To my students, though, far removed from the traumatic events on which it was based, the movie was, well, only a movie. And the thing is, they were right.

Hollywood's involvement with Watergate began in the summer of 1972. Redford was on a whistle-stop tour to promote his newest film, *The Candidate,* when he overheard some press people on the train discussing the break-in. He was struck by their certainty that President Nixon's men were behind it, and that the whole story would never be known. He later noticed that the story did remain largely unreported except for the pieces by Woodward and Bernstein in the *Post.* Then one day he came across an article about the reporting team—about how they were outsiders in the world of Washington journalism, with apparently conflicting personalities. Woodward was a Yalie and registered Republican, Bernstein street-smart and long-haired. "It all clicked," Redford would recall. " 'That's a movie,' I said."[49]

The actor contacted Woodward, learned that the reporters were working on a Watergate book, and set about buying the movie rights. He asked William Goldman, who had written *Butch Cassidy and the Sundance Kid,* the popular 1969 western starring Redford and Paul Newman, to do the script. Given the importance of the subject, Goldman felt that "[g]reat liberties could not be taken with the material.... We had to be dead on, or we were dead."[50] Yet a *Post* editor has described Goldman's first draft as "really nothing more than 'Butch Cassidy and the Sundance Kid Bring Down the Government,' "[51] The screenplay underwent many revisions by many hands.[52] Despite the repeated polishings—or perhaps because of them—Hollywood's fingerprints are all over the final film.

This isn't so much a criticism as a simple observation. It is pointless to criticize a Hollywood film for behaving like a Hollywood film and, in the case of *All the President's Men,* a very successful one. But if you can't argue with success, you can still analyze it. The film was a contemporary retelling of probably the oldest, most central myth of our culture. Alan Pakula, who directed, said the story of "Woodstein" could supplant the Western in film folklore, because its theme is "that American belief that a person or small group can with perseverance and hard work and obsessiveness take on a far more powerful, impersonal body and win—if they have truth on their side."[53]

What stands out about *All the President's Men* is how unshadowed its portrait of the press is, especially when compared with other films or even the original book. Woodward and Bernstein confessed in their best seller to ethical blunders. In the most serious, the reporters approached about half a dozen members of the Watergate grand jury and tried to get them to divulge secret testimony. One of the jurors told a prosecutor about the visit, and the prosecutor told Judge John Sirica. After meeting with the *Post*'s lawyer, Sirica reprimanded the reporters in open court, though he didn't identify them. "They felt lousy," Woodward and Bernstein wrote of themselves in recounting the episode. "They had not broken the law when they had visited the grand jurors, that much seemed certain. But they had sailed around it and exposed others to danger. They had chosen expediency over principle and, caught in the act, their role had been covered up. They had dodged, misrepresented, suggested, and intimidated...."[54]

David Thomson said in *America in the Dark* that a trenchant film would have conveyed the feeling of "the same blurring of scruple at the *Post* and the White House."[55] Alas, that film isn't *All the President's Men.* It either omits or hurries over incidents in Woodward and Bernstein's book that might have reflected badly on the reporters, that might have showed them as anything less than knights-errant. The unbridled professionalism that raises ethical questions—and blood pressures—in anti-press films is given a positive slant. As far as this film is concerned, all's fair in love and investigative reporting.

Woodward and Bernstein barge in where they aren't wanted and sometimes may not belong. "Please go away, OK?" a frightened secretary for the Committee to Reelect the President begs the reporters through a half-open door. "Will you please leave before they see you?" As one might expect in a film by the director of *The Parallax View,* paranoia is epidemic. "Deep Throat" (Hal Holbrook), Woodward's inside source and "garage freak," warns in sepulchral tones that the conspiracy leads everywhere, and that lives are in danger. Trying to pierce the darkness, the reporters trick and harass sources, impersonate officials, spy through windows, and eavesdrop on phone calls. In one scene, Bernstein (Dustin Hoffman) wangles his way into the home of a CREEP bookkeeper (Jane Alexander) and applies all his considerable guile to getting the tense, troubled woman to talk. The film means for us to admire his grit when perhaps we should be deploring his duplicity.

Editors are malevolent creatures in most novels and movies. They teach eager, inexperienced cubs, or reteach temporarily forgetful veterans, the basic rules of the newspaper game: that there are no rules except get the story and get it first. *All the President's Men* keeps the general outline of the sinister stereotype while draining its threatening content. The *Post* editors are mentors and role models, but of a beneficial kind. Metropolitan editor Harry

The *Washington Post* newsroom was re-created at a cost of $200,000 on a sound stage in Burbank, Calif., for the *All the President's Men*. In this scene, Ben Bradlee (Jason Robards, foreground), the *Post*'s executive editor, tells "Woodstein" (Robert Redford, left, and Dustin Hoffman) that they must get harder information next time if they want their story to make the front page. Metropolitan editor Harry Rosenfeld (Jack Warden) stares at the tops of his shoes.

Rosenfeld (Jack Warden) and managing editor Howard Simons (Martin Balsam) take turns delivering homilies on responsible journalism—as they understand it, of course, which isn't too deeply. Both equate the whole of journalistic responsibility with reporting just the facts. "I'm not interested in what you think is obvious. I'm interested in what you know," Rosenfeld tells Bernstein, insisting on a hard-and-fast distinction between thought and knowledge that epistemologists might find laughable, even if my students, in a rare lapse, didn't.

Ben Bradlee (Jason Robards), executive editor of the *Post,* drives Woodward and Bernstein as ruthlessly as any "sultan of slop" ever drove his staff. When the story bogs down, and a frustrated Woodward moans, "We haven't had any luck yet," Bradlee says, with a hint of menace: "Get some." He is grim, imposing, autocratic, able to quash dissent or discussion with a sharp look. But—and it is a big "but"—his mixture of toughness and arrogance always serves the truth. Once he entrusts the story to the "boys," as he calls Woodward and Bernstein with gruff affection, he sticks with them through White House denials, public apathy, and the skepticism of most of the press. The Watergate conspirators are finally no match for his bold generalship.

Or so the film would have us believe. It ignores the contributions of congressional committees and special prosecutors in cracking the cover-up and ends, somewhat abruptly, with a teletypewriter rapping out a series of news flashes: "Hunt pleads guilty . . ."; "Magruder pleads guilty . . ."; "Segretti sentenced . . ."; "Colson pleads guilty . . ."; "Mitchell, Haldeman, Ehrlichman guilty . . ."; "Nixon resigns. . . ." The impression thus created is that the *Post* singlehandedly saved the Constitution. Woodward and Bernstein doubtless deserved their Pulitzer Prize for investigative reporting, but even they had to admit that their work was only a piece, and not the most important one, in a complex puzzle. "[T]he reporters' own stories had only scratched the surface," they wrote in their book, "they did not completely comprehend what had happened and was still happening. . . ."[56]

After Vietnam, Watergate, and the rest, *All the President's Men* raised a new idol, the investigative reporter, on the ruins of old gods and legends. If the film is history, and actual footage of the 1972 presidential campaign is included to suggest that it is, it is history as we might like it to have happened, history with the smooth grain of myth. Everything in the film is larger than life. A nimbus of fear surrounds Washington. The future of the country hangs on the hunches of a couple of kid reporters. It is so clean and simple, so dramatically satisfying, so unlike the real world. Who could ever guess from watching the film that Nixon was pardoned and one day would return, duly anointed by the news media, as an elder statesman, or stranger still, that Gordon Liddy, convicted in the break-in, would make highly publicized guest appearances on *Miami Vice*? The film doesn't show the press as it is, or was, but as it should be, pure of purpose and brave of heart, holding back the night.

## Notes

1. Robert Daley, "Super-Reporter: The Missing American Hero Turns Out To Be ... Clark Kent," *New York*, November 12, 1973, p. 42.

2. Lou Cannon, *Reporting: An Inside View* (Sacramento, Calif.: California Journal Press, 1977), p. 125.

3. Tom Wicker, *On Press* (New York: Viking Press, 1978), p. 15.

4. Leonard Downie, Jr., *The New Muckrakers* (Washington: New Republic, 1976), pp. 7–8.

5. Quoted in Cannon, *Reporting*, p. 53.

6. Chalmers Lowell Pancoast, *Cub* (New York: Devin-Adair, 1928), p. 21.

Around 1880, Charles Edward Russell heard of the detective work done by New York reporters from the tramp printers who passed through his father's newspaper office in Davenport, Iowa. It was clear to him from what they said that "the true glory of newspaper work lay in unraveling murder mysteries. ..." Quoted in Thomas C. Leonard, *The Power of the Press: The Birth of American Political Reporting* (New York: Oxford University Press, 1986), p. 154.

7. Paul H. Weaver, "The New Journalism and the Old—Thoughts after Watergate," *Public Interest* 35 (Spring 1974): 68.

8. Wicker, *On Press,* p. 241.

9. Downie, *New Muckrakers,* p. 9; Michael Schudson, *Discovering the News: A Social History of American Newspapers* (New York: Basic Books, 1978), p. 171.

10. Quoted in Phillip Knightley, *The First Casualty* (New York: Harcourt Brace Jovanovich, 1975), p. 373.

11. Daley, "Super-Reporter," p. 42; Downey, *New Muckrakers,* p. 7.

12. Schudson, *Discovering the News,* pp. 189–90.

13. *Ibid.,* p. 191.

14. Donald Fry, ed., *Believing the News: A Poynter Institute Ethics Center Report* (St. Petersburg, Fla.: Poynter Institute for Media Studies, 1985), p. 54.

15. Downie, *New Muckrakers,* p. 10.

16. *Ibid.*

17. Quoted in Cannon, *Reporting,* p. 289.

18. Quoted in M.L. Stein, "Gloss is taken off investigative reporting," *Editor & Publisher,* October 22, 1983, p. 11.

19. *Ibid.*

20. Fry, *Believing the News,* p. 59.

21. William L. O'Neill, *Coming Apart: An Informal History of America in the 1960's* (New York: Quadrangle Books, 1971), p. 94.

22. Andrew Bergman noticed a similar trend in Depression Era films, which blamed the nation's economic breakdown on "shysters"—politicians and lawyers with silky manners, pencil moustaches, and no scruples. *We're in the Money: Depression America and Its Films* (New York: Harper & Row, 1971), pp. 24, 29.

23. For an excellent discussion of *film noir,* see Michael Wood's chapter, "The Intrepidation of Dreams," in *America in the Movies* (New York: Basic Books, 1975), pp. 97–125.

24. The connection occurred to me while reading Sissela Bok's *Secrets: On the Ethics of Concealment and Revelation* (New York: Pantheon Books, 1982), particularly pp. 4, 32–33, 260–62.

25. John Simon, "From Fake Happyendings to Fake Unhappyendings," *New York Times Magazine,* 8 June 1975, pp. 18–19.

26. *Ibid.,* p. 19.

27. John Howard Griffin, "Preface" to *Black Like Me,* 2nd. ed. (Boston: Houghton Mifflin, 1977), unpaged. The book was originally published in 1960.

28. "Movie Follows True Experiences of Writer," *Ebony,* May 1964, p. 37.

29. Quoted in *ibid.,* p. 38.

30. *Variety Film Reviews, 1964-67,* Vol. 11 (New York: Garland, 1983), unpaged; "Cliché Odessy," *Newsweek,* May 25, 1964, pp. 110B–11B.

31. Richard Schickel, "Paranoid Thriller," *Time,* July 8, 1974, pp. 80–81.

32. Stephen Farber, " 'Conspiracy' Movies," 11 August 1974, *New York Times,* sec. 2, p. 11.

33. Joseph Kanon, "The Parallax Candidate," *Atlantic,* August 1974, pp. 84, 86.

34. *Ibid.,* p. 86.

35. Bok, *Secrets,* p. 32.

36. Quoted in Jane Gross, "Movies and the Press Are an Enduring Romance," 2 June 1985, *New York Times,* sec. 2, p. 19.

37. Jack Kroll, "Beached Whales," *Newsweek,* June 3, 1985, p. 65; Vincent Canby, " 'Fletch,' Starring Chevy Chase, Reporter," 31 May 1985, *New York Times,* sec. 3, p. 10.

38. Thomas Hine, *Populuxe* (New York: Alfred A. Knopf, 1986), p. 177.

39. Quoted in Aljean Harmetz, "Fallout From 'China Syndrome' Has Already Begun," 11 March 1979, *New York Times,* sec. 2, p. 1.

40. Dennis A. Williams, "Beyond 'The China Syndrome,' " *Newsweek,* April 16, 1979, p. 31.

41. Harmetz, "Fallout," p. 1.

42. Aljean Harmetz. "When Nuclear Crisis Imitates a Film," 4 April 1979, *New York Times,* sec. 3, p. 18.

43. Williams, "Beyond 'China Syndrome,' " p. 31.

44. James Carey, "The Dark Continent of American Journalism," in *Reading the News,* ed. by Robert Karl Manoff and Michael Schudson (New York: Pantheon Books, 1986), p. 146.

45. J. Edward Murray, "Quality News Versus Junk News," *Neiman Reports,* Summer 1984, p. 16.

46. Pauline Kael, "The Great White Hope," *New Yorker,* September 9, 1985, p. 73.

47. Aljean Harmetz, "Movie to Have Disclaimer," 30 August 1985, *New York Times,* sec. 3, p. 6.

48. The meteorology comes from Vincent Canby, " 'Flash of Green': a Bribe Amid Honor," 5 October 1984, *New York Times,* sec. 3, p. 14. The film previewed at the New York Film Festival in 1984, but was released in 1985.

49. Seth Cagin and Philip Dray, *Hollywood Films of the Seventies* (New York: Harper & Row, 1984), p. 206.

50. William Goldman, *Adventures in the Screen Trade* (New York: Warner Books, 1983), p. 233.

51. Quoted in Downie, *New Muckrakers,* p. 47.

52. Bernstein and his then-girlfriend Nora Ephron collaborated, to Goldman's dismay, on a completely new script, parts of which were incorporated in the film.

53. Quoted in Downie, *New Muckrakers,* p. 6.

54. Carl Bernstein and Bob Woodward, *All the President's Men* (New York: Simon & Schuster, 1974), p. 224.

55. David Thomson, *America in the Dark: The Impact of Hollywood on American Culture* (New York: William Morrow, 1977), pp. 259–60.

56. Bernstein and Woodward, *All the President's Men,* p. 249.

# EPILOGUE: DARK ADAPTATION

> We shall not cease from exploration
> And the end of all our exploring
> Will be to arrive where we started
> And know the place for the first time.
> —T.S. Eliot, "Little Gidding"

WHILE THE DEMISE OF the movie industry has been predicted time and again, Hollywood has always managed to confound the doomsayers.[1] Movies have survived the Great Depression, wars, the introduction of TV, the flight to the suburbs—fundamental changes in technology, economics, and demographics.[2] If the past is any guide, there is little reason to think that movies will disappear in the foreseeable future. What may disappear, however, is the social experience of moviegoing.

The cause would be the videocassette recorder, which by the end of 1987 was installed in 50 percent of American homes.[3] All age groups seem to prefer watching movies at home to watching them in theaters.[4] "With the VCR," as Gary Gumpert pointed out, "crowds are avoided, lines are unnecessary, and the cost per viewing is far less than the price of a ticket."[5] A survey sponsored by Columbia Pictures/Coca Cola found that theater attendance fell to 100 million in 1985, from 113 million in 1983. By comparison, about 25.7 million VCR owners rented an average of four movies each month, up from 1.8 movies each month in 1983.[6] To put it plainly, the "film experience is becoming a private experience."[7]

For those of us who grew up on Saturday matinees and who took high-school dates to the movies, lasciviously holding hands with a girl in the aphrodisiac dark, the disappearance of neighborhood theaters is a sad thing. Another link to the past has been severed, another social interaction diminished. When I close my eyes, I can still see the tattered velvet ropes in the lobby of the Gables, the high, curved ceiling of the theater decorated with plaster fruit and flowers, the dust angels dancing in the beam of light from the projection booth. It was a world of faded splendor, and now more than ever it speaks to me of the impermanence of life.

Old theaters are torn down or converted to churches of obscure denominations or simply stand abandoned, but movies continue to thrive, because Americans continue to need their fantasies. Indications are that the journalist will remain a salient figure in these for some time to come. *Street Smart,* about an opportunistic magazine writer who fabricates a story, was released in the spring of 1987. Late that year, writer-director James L. Brooks combined romantic comedy with *Network*-like parody in the critically and commercially successful *Broadcast News.* Meanwhile, *Brenda Starr,* featuring Brooke Shields as the magenta-haired reporter of comic-strip fame, completed shooting, and *Fletch II* was scheduled for production.[8]

As long as the press shapes our consciousness, Hollywood will be drawn to tell stories about it. "In a world where the news media provide so much of our information about what lies beyond our ken . . . ," Robert Karl Manoff and Michael Schudson said, "it is important to read not only the news, but journalists and journalism itself."[9] Journalism films offer the public a vision of how a great and powerful institution operates. The vision may be distorted, it may be melodramatic, it may be superficial, it may be unfair. None of that really matters, though, if it seems to explain why things are the way they are.

Looking up a word in the dictionary the other day, I happened to notice at the bottom of the page the phrase "dark adaptation." It was one of those instances of serendipity that all researchers know and perhaps secretly depend on. The phrase refers to "the reflex adaptation of the eye to dim light, consisting of a dilatation of the pupil and an increase in the number of functioning rods accompanied by a decrease in the number of functioning cones."

Dark adaptation occurs when the lights go down in the theater, and we lift eager eyes to the screen. But the dictionary definition wasn't what struck me. I was struck, rather, by the ghostly sound of the phrase, its mysterious melancholia, the shadows clinging to the soft folds of its syllables. There is something about it that evokes for me the power of movies to synthesize and mythologize, to transform history into fables and longings into formulas. Movies, with their exaggerations and evasions, help us adapt to the darkness in our lives.

The image of journalists in contemporary film emerges from the maelstrom of American culture. It reflects the tensions between tradition and progress, between nature and technology, between personal morality and professional ethics, all filtered through genre rules, which themselves evolve according to time and chance. We enter the universe of journalism films as we enter a dream, surrendering to feelings we can neither face in daylight nor entirely disavow.[10] The journalist embodies the innocence we mock, the death we worship, the beauty we destroy. Whether portrayed as a cynic or idealist, a scandalmonger or crusader, he absorbs our pain, fear, rage, doubt, and then diffuses them in the golden fluorescence of a fantasy.

"What else we gonna live by if not dreams?" novelist Jill Robinson, the daughter of a former Hollywood producer, rhetorically asked. "We need to believe in something. What would really drive us crazy is to believe this reality we run into every day is all there is."[11] Yet I am strangely elated to be turning now from the illusions of film and back to the real world. I have wandered too long among the mirages and magic shows of the mass media. Perhaps we all have. Newspapers and movies, magazines and TV, surround us with images that reflect cultural values and attitudes more than reality. "We'll tell you any shit you want to hear," Howard Beale, the "mad prophet" of *Network* (1976), declared.[12] I find myself choking on the stench.

And so I leave that carnival of gruesome headlines and smirking newscasters and gaudy Hollywood fantasies.

The end of all my exploring has been to arrive where I started and know the place for the first time. My wife's breasts swell with sweet milk. There are toys on the grass, and poems and explosions in the garden. Birds flash like arrows through the yard. At dusk, the woods behind the house fill with purple and the noise of amorous peepers. Windows bloom with light, stars leap into the sky—everything leaps and blooms as if to welcome me home.

## *Notes*

1. Garth Jowett and James M. Linton, *Movies as Mass Communication* (Beverly Hills, Calif.: Sage, 1980), pp. 113–14.

2. I might have added to this already long list the Hollywood sex scandals of the 1920s, the most infamous being Fatty Arbuckle's in 1921. "Involving murder and rape at a show-folk orgy, the scandal inspired over a hundred legislative bills calling for film censorship, a ban on all movies by one town in Massachusetts, and a foundation for the anti-Hollywood sentiment around the country." Sidney D. Kirkpatrick, *A Cast of Killers* (New York: Penguin Books, 1986), p. 36.

The House Un-American Activities Committee's investigations of communism in Hollywood in the late 1940s and early 1950s posed still another threat to the film industry. The studios reacted to it with all the courage of which they were capable: they blacklisted politically suspect writers, directors, and actors. Otto Friedrich, *City of Nets: A Portrait of Hollywood in the 1940's* (New York: Harper & Row, 1986), pp. 291–337; Victor S. Navasky, *Naming Names* (New York: Penguin Books, 1981).

3. Hans Fantel, "The Year the VCR Became Ubiquitous," *New York Times,* 27 December 1987, sec. 2, p. 26.

4. Tom Green, "Fans tune in VCRs, tune out theaters," *USA Today,* 15 May 1986, p. 1.

5. Gary Gumpert, *Talking Tombstones and Other Tales of the Media Age* (New York: Oxford University Press, 1987), p. 181.

6. Green, "Fans tune in VCRs," p. 1.

7. Gumpert, *Talking Tombstones,* p. 181.

8. The release of *Brenda Starr,* originally scheduled for early 1988, was postponed, perhaps indefinitely.

9. Robert Karl Manoff and Michael Schudson, "Reading the News," in *Reading the News,* ed. by Manoff and Schudson (New York: Pantheon Books, 1986), p. 8.

10. I am paraphrasing Michael Wood, who wrote that popular movies "permit us to look without looking at things we can neither fully face nor entirely disavow." *America in the Movies* (New York: Basic Books, 1975), p. 163.

11. Quoted in Studs Terkel, *American Dreams: Lost and Found* (New York: Pantheon Books, 1980), p. 61.

12. Lewis H. Lapham expressed the same idea more elegantly. "If the media succeed with their spectacles and grand simplifications," he said, "it is because their audiences define happiness as the state of being well and artfully deceived. People like to listen to stories, to believe what they are told.... The media thus play the part of courtier, reassuring their patrons that the world conforms to the wish of the presiding majority." "Gilding the News," *Harper's,* July 1981, p. 37.

# BIBLIOGRAPHY


Adair, Gilbert. *Vietnam on Film.* N.p.: Proteus, 1981.

Adams, Samuel Hopkins. *The Clarion.* New York: Grosset & Dunlap, 1914.

__________. *Success.* Boston: Houghton Mifflin, 1919.

Adler, Renata. *Reckless Disregard: Westmoreland v. CBS et al.; Sharon v. Time.* New York: Alfred A. Knopf, 1986.

Affron, Charles. *Cinema and Sentiment.* Chicago: University of Chicago Press, 1982.

Alloway, Lawrence. *Violent America: The Movies, 1946-1964.* New York: Museum of Modern Art, 1971.

Altsheler, Joseph A. *Gutherie of the Times.* New York: Doubleday, Page, 1904.

Arlen, Michael. *The Living-Room War.* New York: Viking Press, 1969.

Bach, Stephen. *Final Cut: Dreams and Disaster in the Making of Heaven's Gate.* New York: Morrow, 1985.

Bagdikian, Ben H. *The Effete Conspiracy.* New York: Harper & Row, 1972.

__________. *The Media Monopoly.* Boston: Beacon Press, 1983.

Barris, Alex. *Stop the Presses!: The Newspaperman in American Films.* South Brunswick, N.J.: A.S. Barnes, 1976.

Barthes, Roland. *Mythologies.* Selected and translated by Annette Levers. New York: Hill and Wang, 1972.

Benjamin, Burton. "TV Network News Finds the Rules Have Changed." *New York Times,* 17 August 1986, sec. 2, pp. 1, 25.

Bergman, Andrew. *We're in the Money: Depression America and Its Films.* New York: Harper & Row, 1971.

Berman, Janice. "The Latest Edition." *Newsday,* 9 November 1986, part II, pp. 4–5.

Bernstein, Carl, and Woodward, Bob. *All the President's Men.* New York: Simon & Schuster, 1974.

Bessie, Simon Michael. *Jazz Journalism.* New York: Dutton, 1938; reprint ed., New York: Russel & Russel, 1969.

Bok, Sissela. *Secrets: On the Ethics of Concealment and Revelation.* New York: Pantheon Books, 1982.

Boot, William. "Iranscam: when the cheering stopped." *Columbia Journalism Review,* March/April 1987, pp. 20–25.

Boylan, James. "Declarations of Independence." *Columbia Journalism Review,* November/December 1986, pp. 29–45.

Brush, Katharine. *Young Man of Manhattan.* New York: Farrar & Rinehart, 1930.

Bullard, F. Lauriston. *Famous War Correspondents.* Boston: Little, Brown, 1914.

Burstein, Daniel. "I dreamed I saw Pol Pot last night." *Quill,* May 1982, pp. 17–19.

Cagin, Seth, and Dray, Philip. *Hollywood Films of the Seventies.* New York: Harper & Row, 1984.

Cannon, Lou. *Reporting: An Inside View.* Sacramento, Calif.: California Journal Press, 1977.

Caputo, Philip. *DelCorso's Gallery.* New York: Rinehart and Winston, 1983.

Carey, James W. "A Plea for the University Tradition." Presidential address to American Educators in Journalism. Seattle, Wash., August 13, 1978.

Cavell, Stanley. *The World Viewed: Reflections on the Ontology of Film.* Enlarged ed. Cambridge: Harvard University Press, 1979.

Christian, Shirley. "Covering the Sandinistas." *Washington Journalism Review,* March 1982, pp. 33–38.

Christians, Clifford G.; Rotzoll, Kim B.; and Fackler, Mark. *Media Ethics: Cases and Moral Reasoning.* New York: Longman, 1983.

Churchill, Allen. *Park Row.* New York: Rinehart, 1958.

Clarens, Carlos. *Crime Movies: From Griffith to The Godfather and Beyond.* New York: W.W. Norton, 1981.

"A Conversation with Neil Postman: TV 'Has Culture by the Throat.' " *U.S. News & World Reports,* December 23, 1985, pp. 57–58.

Cook, Fred J. *Maverick: Fifty Years of Investigative Reporting.* New York: G.P. Putnam's Sons, 1984.

Corliss, Richard. "Backing into the Future," *Time,* February 3, 1986, pp. 64–65.

Crawford, Remsen. "Aces of the Press." *North American Review,* January 1929, pp. 109–16.

Crane, Stephen. *Active Service.* New York: International Association of Newspapers & Authors, 1901.

"Credibility." *Bulletin of the American Society of Newspaper Editors,* March 1982, pp. 3–21.

Cross, Donna Woolfolk. *Mediaspeak: How Television Makes Up Your Mind.* New York: New American Library, 1983.

Daley, Robert. "Super-Reporter: The Missing American Hero Turns Out To Be... Clark Kent." *New York,* November 12, 1973, pp. 42–48.

Davis, Richard Harding. *The Galloper.* In *Farces.* New York: Charles Scribner's Sons, 1906.

_________. *Gallegher and Other Stories.* New York: Charles Scribner's Sons, 1904.

"Dere Press Corps: Drop Dead." *Washington Journalism Review.* March 1987, p. 14.

Diamond, Edwin. "The Best and the Blandest: Who's Who in Journalism." *New York,* March 31, 1986, pp. 19–20.

_________. *The Tin Kazoo: Television, Politics, and the News.* Cambridge, Mass.: MIT Press, 1975.

Didion, Joan. "In Hollywood." In *White Album.* New York: Simon and Schuster, 1979, pp. 153–67.

Downie, Leonard, Jr. *The New Muckrakers.* Washington: New Republic, 1976.

Dreiser, Theodore. "Out of My Newspaper Days." *Bookman,* Vol. LIV, September 1921-February 1922, pp. 208–17, 427–33, 542–50.

Dunne, John. *The Studio.* New York: Farrar, Straus & Giroux, 1969.

Ellerbee, Linda. *And So It Goes.* New York: Berkley Books, 1986.

Emery, Edwin, and Emery, Michael. *The Press and America: An Interpretive History of the Mass Media.* 5th ed. Englewood Cliffs, N.J.: Prentice-Hall, 1984.

Epstein, Edward J. *Between Fact and Fiction: The Problems of Journalism.* New York: Vintage Books, 1975.

Evans, Katherine Winton. "National Security and the Press." *Washington Journalism Review,* July 1986, pp. 14-17.

Fabrikant, Geraldine. "Not Ready for Prime Time." *New York Times Magazine,* 12 April 1987, pp. 30–37.

_________. "Ted Turner's Screen Test." *New York Times,* 30 March 1985, sec. 3, pp. 1, 8.

Fenin, George N., and Everson, William K., *The Western: From Silents to the Seventies.* New York: Grossman, 1973.

Ferber, Edna. *Cimarron.* Greenwich, Conn.: Fawcett, 1971.

Fetherling, Doug. *The Five Lives of Ben Hecht.* Canada: Lester and Orpen, 1977.

Fiedler, Leslie. *A Fiedler Reader.* New York: Stein and Day, 1977.

Fine, Richard. *Hollywood and the Profession of Authorship, 1928–1940.* Ann Arbor, Mich.: UMI Research Press, 1985.

Fitzgerald, F. Scott. *The Last Tycoon.* New York: Charles Scribner's Sons, 1941.

Franks, Lucinda. "Hollywood Update." *Columbia Journalism Review,* November/December 1981, pp. 59, 61, 63.

Friedrich, Otto. *City of Nets: A Portrait of Hollywood in the 1940's.* New York: Harper & Row, 1986.

Friedman, Lester D. *Hollywood's Image of the Jew.* New York: Frederick Ungar, 1982.

Fry, Don, ed. *Believing the News: A Poynter Institute Ethics Center Report.* St. Petersburg, Fla.: Poynter Institute for Media Studies, 1985.

Fuller, Sam. "News That's Fit to Film." *American Film,* I:1 (October 1975): 20–24.

Furneaux, Rupert. *The First War Correspondent: William Howard Russell of the Times.* London: Cassell, 1945.

Fussell, Paul. *The Great War and Modern Memory.* London: Oxford University Press, 1975.

Garnham, Nicholas. *Sam Fuller.* New York: Viking Press, 1971.

Gitlin, Todd, ed. *Watching Television.* New York: Pantheon Books, 1986.

Goldman, William. *Adventures in the Screen Trade.* New York: Warner Books, 1983.

Good, Howard. *Acquainted with the Night: The Image of Journalists in American Fiction, 1890–1930.* Metuchen, N.J.: Scarecrow Press, 1986.

________. "The Image of Journalism in American Poetry." *American Journalism,* IV: 3 (1987): 123–132.

________. "The Image of War Correspondents in Anglo-American Fiction." *Journalism Monographs,* no. 97, July 1986.

Goodman, Walter. "Why Some Novelists Cast Hollywood As the Heavy." *New York Times,* 17 August 1986, sec. 2, pp. 19–20.

Goodwin, H. Eugene. *Groping for Ethics in Journalism.* Ames: Iowa State University Press, 1983.

Greene, Graham. *The Quiet American.* London: William Heinemann, 1955; reprint ed., New York: Penguin Books, 1981.

Griffin, John Howard. *Black Like Me.* 2nd ed. Boston: Houghton Mifflin, 1977.

Gross, Jane. "Movies and the Press Are an Enduring Romance." *New York Times,* 2 June 1985, sec. 2, pp. 1, 19.

Gumpert, Gary. *Talking Tombstones and Other Tales of the Media Age.* New York: Oxford University Press, 1987.

Harrison, Henry Sydnor. *Queed.* Boston: Houghton Mifflin, 1911.

Haskell, Molly. *From Reverence to Rape: The Treatment of Women in the Movies.* New York: Rinehart and Winston, 1974.

Henry, William A., III. "Journalism Under Fire." *Time,* December 12, 1983, pp. 76–93.

Hereford, William Richard. *The Demagog.* New York: Henry Holt, 1909.

Herr, Michael. *Dispatches.* New York: Avon Books, 1978.

Hine, Thomas. *Populuxe.* New York: Alfred A. Knopf, 1986.

Isaacs, Norman E. *Untended Gates: The Mismanaged Press.* New York: Columbia University Press, 1986.

Jarvie, Ian. "The Social Experience of Movies." In *Film/Culture: Explorations in Cinema in its Social Context.* Edited by Sari Thomas. Metuchen, N.J.: Scarecrow Press, 1982, pp. 247–68.

Jones, Alex S. "The Anchors." *New York Times Magazine,* 27 July 1986, pp. 13–17, 22–24.

Jowett, Garth, and Linton, James M. *Movies as Mass Communication.* Beverly Hills, Calif.: Sage, 1980.

Just, Ward. *The American Blues.* New York: Viking Press, 1984.

Kael, Pauline. *The Citizen Kane Book.* Boston: Little, Brown, 1971.

__________. "Trash, Art, and the Movies." In *Going Steady.* Boston: Little, Brown, 1970.

Katzenbach, John. *In the Heat of the Summer.* New York: Ballantine, 1982.

Keegan, John. *The Face of War.* New York: Viking Press, 1976.

Keyser, Les. *Hollywood in the Seventies.* San Diego: A.S. Barnes, 1981.

Kipling, Rudyard. *The Light That Failed.* New York: H.M. Caldwell, 1899.

Kirkhorn, Michael J. "The Virtuous Journalist: An Exploratory Essay." *Quill,* February 1982, pp. 9–23.

Kirkpatrick, Sidney D. *A Cast of Killers.* New York: Penguin Books. 1986.

Knightley, Phillip. *The First Casualty.* New York: Harcourt, Brace, Javanovich, 1975.

Lapham, Lewis H. "Gilding the News." *Harper's,* July 1981, pp. 31–39.

Lasch, Christopher. *The Culture of Narcissism: American Life in an Age of Diminishing Expectations.* New York: Warner Books, 1979.

Lawrence, D.H. *Studies in Classic American Literature.* New York: Viking Press, 1964.

Leonard, Thomas C. *The Power of the Press: The Birth of American Political Reporting.* New York: Oxford University Press, 1986.

Levy, Mark R., and Robinson, John. "The 'huh?' factor: untangling TV news." *Columbia Journalism Review,* July/August 1986, pp. 48–49.

Lukas, J. Anthony. *Nightmare: The Underside of the Nixon Years.* New York: Bantam, 1977.

Lyman, Olin L. *Micky.* Boston: Richard G. Badger, 1905.

McConnell, Frank D. *The Spoken Seen: Film and the Romantic Imagination.* Baltimore: Johns Hopkins University Press, 1975.

McCullough, Francis. "The Question of the War Correspondent." *Contemporary Review,* CIII, February 1913, pp. 203–13.

MacLean, Charles Agnew. *The Mainspring.* Boston: Little, Brown, 1912.

McPhaul, John J. *Deadlines & Monkeyshines: The Fabled World of Chicago Journalism.* Englewood Cliffs, N.J.: Prentice-Hall, 1962.

Manoff, Robert Karl, and Schudson, Michael, eds. *Reading the News.* New York: Pantheon Books, 1986.

Mathews, Joseph P. *Reporting the Wars.* Minneapolis: University of Minnesota Press, 1957.

Matthews, Herbert L. *The Education of a Correspondent.* New York: Harcourt, Brace, 1956.

Matusow, Barbara. *The Evening Stars: The Making of the Network News Anchors.* Boston: Houghton Mifflin, 1983.

Mellett, John C. *Ink.* Indianapolis: Bobbs-Merrill, 1930.

Michelson, Miriam. *A Yellow Journalist.* New York: Appleton, 1905.

"Mirror, mirror on the wall. . . . " *Columbia Journalism Review,* March/April 1986, p. 24.

Morgan, Thomas. "Reporters of the Lost War." *Esquire,* July 1984, pp. 51–60.

Murray, J. Edward. "Quality News Versus Junk News." *Neiman Reports,* Summer 1984, pp. 14–19.

Navasky, Victor S. *Naming Names.* New York: Penguin Books, 1981.

O'Connor, John, J. "Television Tests Its Limits." *New York Times,* 11 October 1987, sec. 2, pp. 1, 35.

_________. "The 'Vast Wasteland,' 25 Years After." *New York Times,* 4 May 1986, sec. 2, pp. 1, 29.

O'Neill, William L. *Coming Apart: An Informal History of America in the 1960s.* New York: Quadrangle Books, 1971.

Palmer, Frederick. *With My Own Eyes.* Indianapolis: Bobbs-Merrill, 1933.

Pancoast, Chalmers Lowell. *Cub.* New York: Devin-Adair, 1928.

Pattison, Robert. *On Literacy: The Politics of the Word from Homer to the Age of Rock.* New York: Oxford University Press, 1982.

Peck, Abe. *Uncovering the Sixties: The Life and Times of the Underground Press.* New York: Pantheon Books, 1985.

*The People & The Press: A Times Mirror Investigation of Public Attitudes Toward the News Media, Conducted by the Gallup Organization.* Los Angeles: Times Mirror, 1986.

Phelan, John M. *Disenchantment: Meaning and Morality in the Media.* New York: Hastings House, 1980.

Phillips, David Graham. *The Great God Success.* New York: Grosset & Dunlap, 1901; reprint ed., Ridgewood, N.J.: Gregg Press, 1967.

Postman, Neil. *Amusing Ourselves to Death.* New York: Viking Press, 1985.

Powdermaker, Hortense. *Hollywood the Dream Factory: An Anthropologist Looks at Movie-Makers.* Boston: Little, Brown, 1950.

Quart, Leonard, and Auster, Albert. *American Film and Society Since 1945.* New York: Praeger, 1984.

Rollins, Peter C., ed. *Hollywood As Historian: American Film in a Cultural Context.* Lexington: University Press of Kentucky, 1983.

Rosenbaum, Ron. "The Reel Scoop." *Mademoiselle,* June 1985, pp. 66–67.

Ross, Lillian. *Picture.* In *Reporting.* New York: Simon and Schuster, 1969.

Ross, Malcolm. *Penny Dreadful.* New York: Coward-McCann, 1929.

Rossell, Deac. "Hollywood and the Newsroom." *American Film,* I:1 (October 1975): 14–18.

Rothmeyer, Karen. "Hot properties: the media-buying spree explained." *Columbia Journalism Review,* November/December 1985, pp. 38–43.

Ruth, Marcia, "Covering Foreign News." *Presstime,* April 1986, pp. 35–38.

Ryan, Desmond. "The Hollywood Reporter." *Washington Journalism Review,* September 1985, pp. 45–47.

Sanoff, Alvin P. "Behind Wave of Libel Suits Hitting Nation's Press." *U.S. News & World Report,* November 5, 1984, pp. 53–54.

Sayre, Nora. "Falling Prey to Parodies of the Press." In *New York Times Encyclopedia of Film.* New York: Times Books, 1984.

__________. *Running Time: Films of the Cold War.* New York: Dial Press, 1982.

Schanberg, Sydney H. *The Death and Life of Dith Pran.* New York: Penguin Books, 1985.

Schatz, Thomas. *Hollywood Genres: Formulas, Filmmaking, and the Studio System.* New York: Random House, 1981.

Schickel, Richard. *Intimate Strangers: The Culture of Celebrity.* New York: Doubleday, 1985.

Schudson, Michael. *Discovering the News: A Social History of American Newspapers.* New York: Basic Books, 1978.

Schulberg, Budd. *The Disenchanted.* New York: Random House, 1950.

__________. *Moving Pictures: Memories of a Hollywood Prince.* New York: Stein and Day, 1981.

Shadoian, Jack. *Dreams and Dead Ends: The American Gangster/Crime Film.* Cambridge, Mass.: MIT Press, 1977.

Shaw, David. "On Arrogance and Accountability in the Press." Address presented at the University of Hawaii, March 8, 1983.

__________. *Press Watch.* New York: Macmillan, 1984.

Shawcross, William. *Sideshow: Kissinger, Nixon and the Destruction of Cambodia.* New York: Pocket Books, 1979.

Sherrill, Robert. "News Ethics: Press & Jerks." *Grand Street,* Winter 1986, pp. 115–133.

Shirer, William L. *20th Century Journey: The Nightmare Years, 1930–1940.* Vol. 2. Boston: Little, Brown, 1984.

Shuman, Edwin L. *Practical Journalism.* New York: Appleton, 1903.

Simon, John. "From Fake Happyendings to Fake Unhappyendings." *New York Times Magazine,* 8 June 1975, pp. 18–35.

Sklar, Robert. *Movie-Made America.* New York: Random House, 1975.

Slotkin, Richard. "Myth and the Production of History." In *Ideology and Classic American Literature.* Edited by Sacvan Bercovitch and Myra Jehlen. Cambridge: Cambridge University Press, 1986, pp. 70–90.

———. "Prologue to a Study of Myth and Genre in American Movies." In *Prospects: The Annual of American Cultural Studies.* Vol. 9. Edited by Jack Salzman. Cambridge: Cambridge University Press, 1984, pp. 407–32.

Smith, Henry Justin. *Deadlines.* Chicago: Covici-McGee, 1923.

Sobchack, Vivian. "Genre Film: Myth, Ritual, and Sociodrama." In *Film/Culture: Explorations of Cinema in its Social Context.* Edited by Sari Thomas. Metuchen, N.J.: Scarecrow Press, 1982, pp. 147-65.

Spewack, Bella and Samuel. *Clear All Wires.* New York: French, 1932.

Stark, Steven D. "10 Years into the Stallone Era: What It, Uh, All Means." *New York Times,* 22 February 1987, sec. 2, pp. 19, 21.

Stein, M.L. " 'Gloss' is taken off investigative reporting." *Editor & Publisher,* October 22, 1983, pp. 10–11.

———. *Under Fire: The Story of American War Correspondents.* New York: Messner, 1968.

Stoler, Peter. *The War Against the Press: Politics, Pressure and Intimidation in the 80's.* New York: Dodd, Mead, 1986.

Tarkington, Booth. *The Gentleman from Indiana.* New York: Charles Scribner's Sons, 1915.

Teague, Bob. *Live and Off Color: News Biz.* New York: A & W Publishers, 1982.

Terkel, Studs. *American Dreams: Lost and Found.* New York: Pantheon Books, 1980.

Thomson, David. *America in the Dark: The Impact of Hollywood on American Culture.* New York: William Morrow, 1977.

Trachtenberg, Alan. "Myth and Symbol." *Massachusetts Review* (Winter 1984): 667–73.

Tuska, Jon. *The Detective in Hollywood.* Garden City, N.Y.: Doubleday, 1978.

Twitchell, James R. *Dreadful Pleasures: An Anatomy of Modern Horror.* New York: Oxford University Press, 1985.

Umphlett, Wiley Lee. *The Movies Go to College: Hollywood and the World of the College-Life Film.* Cranbury, N.J.: Associated University Presses, 1984.

Walker, Stanley. *City Editor.* New York: Frederick A. Stokes, 1934.

Wallace, Irving. *The Almighty.* Garden City, N.Y.: Doubleday, 1982.

Ward, Alex. "David Rayfiel's Script Magic." *New York Times Magazine,* 6 April 1986, pp. 24–29, 38.

Warshow, Robert. *The Immediate Experience.* New York: Atheneum, 1975.

Waters, Harry F. "Prime Time for Vietnam." *Newsweek,* August 31, 1987, pp. 68–69.

Weales, Gerald. *Canned Goods as Caviar: American Film Comedy of the 1930s.* Chicago: University of Chicago Press, 1985.

Weaver, Paul H. "The New Journalism and the Old—Thoughts After Watergate." *Public Interest,* no. 35, Spring 1974, pp. 67–88.

Weiss, Philip. "The Invasion of the Gannettoids." *New Republic,* February 2, 1987, pp. 16–22.

Wicker, Tom. *On Press.* New York: Viking Press, 1978.

Williams, Alan. "Is a Radical Genre Criticism Possible?" *Quarterly Review of Film Studies,* Spring 1984, pp. 121–25.

Williams, Ben Ames. *Splendor.* New York: Dutton, 1927.

Williams, Jesse Lynch. *The Day-Dreamer.* New York: Doubleday, Page, 1906.

Wilson, James C. *Vietnam in Prose and Film.* Jefferson, N.C.: McFarland, 1982.

Wines, Michael. "Burnout in the Newsroom." *Washington Journalism Review,* May 1986, pp. 35–38.

Wolfe, Tom. "The New Journalism." In *The New Journalism.* Edited by Tom Wolfe and E.W. Johnson. New York: Harper & Row, 1970.

Wood, Michael. *America in the Movies.* New York: Basic Books, 1975.

Zynda, Thomas H. "The Hollywood Version: Movie Portrayals of the Press." *Journalism History* 6:1 (Spring 1978): 16–25, 32.

I consulted the following newspapers and magazines for film reviews and related articles:

*Atlantic*

*Ebony*

*Life*

*Mademoiselle*

*Nation*

*New Republic*

*New York*

*New York Times*

*New Yorker*

*Newsweek*

*People*

*Saturday Review*

*Time*

*USA Today*

*Variety*

# INDEX